Morgan St. John

About the Author

In 2001, Adam Ginsberg was the owner of a small pool table business who decided to try selling his pool tables on eBay. In less than one year, he became the number one seller in the Sports category, and then was named eBay's number one new seller in 2002. He has had sales months in excess of one million dollars in merchandise. Adam has personally sold over $20,000,000 on eBay in the last three years, his feedback score is consistently averaged at 99.60 percent, and he is a Titanium PowerSeller, eBay's highest level.

Adam, who graduated from Tulane University with a Bachelor of Science in management and a minor in psychology, is also a popular public speaker with the Learning Annex, America's top seminar chain. Born in Brooklyn, New York, Ginsberg now lives in Los Angeles, California.

How to
Buy, Sell
& Profit
on eBay

How to Buy, Sell & Profit on eBay

Kick-Start Your Home-Based Business in Just Thirty Days

ADAM GINSBERG

HARPER

NEW YORK • LONDON • TORONTO • SYDNEY

HARPER

HarperCollins books may be purchased for educational, business, or sales promotional use. For information please write: Special Markets Department, HarperCollins Publishers Inc., 10 East 53rd Street, New York, NY 10022.

FIRST COLLINSLIFESTYLE EDITION PUBLISHED 2005.

Library of Congress Cataloging-in-Publication Data

Ginsberg, Adam.
How to buy, sell, and profit on ebay : kick-start your home-based business in just thirty days / Adam Ginsberg.—1st ed.
p. cm.
ISBN 0-06-076287-X (trade pbk. : alk. paper)
1. ebay (Firm). 2. Internet auctions. 3. Small business—Management. 4. New business enterprises. I. Title.

HF5478.G56 2005
658.8'7—dc22   2004060023

11 12 13 14 ❖/RRD 20 19 18 17 16

To my mom, who for most of my life was my support system and best friend. It was her passion and unconditional belief in me, that motivated me to get involved in this business. She was there, every step of the way, through the good and the bad times to provide guidance and inspiration.

Recently she passed away unexpectedly. Fortunately she had a chance to review the manuscript and give me one last stamp of approval. She was so excited about this book and about life in general. She loved eBay and she loved her family.

Mom, you have left this place at such an untimely moment and I miss you more than words can express. This book is for you and your spirit will continue to live through each page. I will continue to share your eBay—and life—passions with everyone I come in contact with.

I love you, I miss you, and I thank you from the bottom of my heart.

Acknowledgments

How does a person say "thank you" when there are so many people to thank? Two people come to mind: my dad, for being a powerful role model; and Maureen O'Brien, my editor, who had the belief in me and the vision to see this project through to completion.

The person most directly responsible for this becoming a reality is my wife, Jennifer, who makes my life complete. Jennifer is my partner in marriage, business, and in life. For Jennifer's incredible patience, support, and understanding, each morning I "pulled the laptop out from under the bed" to check my e-mail and listings. Without her I would be lost. To Howard and Iris for raising such a great daughter. For my daughter, Haley, who always understands "one more minute" before we leave for school or the park while I check my feedback or return a call—and her acceptance that it's never just "one more minute." I am blessed to have an incredibly supportive family, and I love them all! I thank Don Freda for being my incredible mentor and role model; to Bill Zanker, Steven Schragis, and the entire Learning Annex Team for making this book happen. I thank James Burgin for his wisdom and inspiration; and his Brand

Within Team: Diane Kennedy, and everyone who contributed to Fast Cash on eBay; Edie and Britanni for being instrumental in the flow of the book; Robert Campbell for being my best friend; Jeff Vikari for his incredible energy and encouragement; Robert Sheman for his insights into the seminar business; Chris Bryant for being there with me every day and providing much-needed support; again to Maureen O'Brien for her passion; Angela Fok, Chad Mah, Paul Rees, Lou Ferris, Brian Pentecost, Joe Cardillo, Liz Gayford, Dominic Palladino, Tony Sibbald, Erick Laine, Bruce Goodman, and Joe Grushkin for an incredible foundation in business philosophy and teamwork, and the thousands of graduates of Buy, Sell & Profit on eBay seminars. Finally, this book would not have been possible without the interactions with the great buyers and sellers that make up the eBay marketplace. It is these real-life experiences that keep me grounded.

Contents

Part Four: Taking It to the Next Level

Cracking the Code

Tuesday, October 23, 2001
1:30 a.m.

Eleven minutes and thirty-six seconds to go, and I'm about to part with a brand-new, eight-foot, hand-carved, solid-mahogany pool table for $165. The item retails for $1,950 at my store in Culver City. This is going to be a total loss.

Thank God.

It's worth at least the difference to shut my mother up once and for all about this eBay hokey-pokey nonsense. She thinks that just because she's buying and selling Beanie Babies on eBay all day she knows what's best for my business. Well, in exactly eleven minutes, I'm going to show her who, in fact, knows what's best for my business. And it ain't Sheila Ginsberg.

Oh, look, there's another bid. It's up to a whopping $170. I'm in business.

Yeah, right. The calls started about a month ago. My

mother phoned and said she had a great idea for me that might help me out. "You should start selling your pool tables on eBay." You've seen a pool table, yes? They weigh a thousand pounds. Every part comes separately—pockets, felt, all of it—and it all needs to be set up wherever it's going to stay. She was out of her mind.

"OK, Mom. I'll look into it."

I very quickly dismissed the conversation and, as any devoted son would do, I ignored her.

Hold on for a moment, let me refresh the screen just for—holy cow! The high bid just shot up to $400 in two minutes.

Well, maybe I'll get to cover my shipping costs. Come to think of it, I don't even know how much it costs to ship a pool table. I don't even know *how* to ship a pool table.

Regardless, I moved on with my life, and then, a few days later, Mom called back. "So Adam, tell me about the listing of the pool table on eBay, how's it going?"

I told her I had no idea what she was talking about.

"You know, the pool table you told me you'd list."

Did I say that? "I didn't say that."

This conversation went on for weeks and—I don't believe it! It's up to $1,050! This is absolutely insane! I've got to lay off this F5 key. Every time I press it, the screen refreshes and tells me if new bids have been made—and I can't stop myself from checking!

So, my mother, she'd call me again and again and completely ignore everything I had said the last time. "How much did it sell for?" "How did you ship it?" She was absolutely relentless.

Exactly three days ago, last Saturday the twentieth, I woke up at one in the morning and I couldn't go back to sleep. My mother's voice kept echoing in my head, "eBay this thing, eBay that thing, eBay the other thing." I sat up and went straight for the computer. I had to get her off my—this can't be right. There is no way that someone just bid $1,200 for my pool table. Suddenly four minutes left seems like an eternity.

Let me finish my story . . . although, I have to tell you, it's starting to get hard to concentrate on anything else right now but this pool table listing on my laptop screen. Let me just hit F5 one more time—$1,400. Twenty seconds and $200! No more F5. Let this go, Adam.

As I was saying, I had moved three thousand miles to get away from home and now I can't get her out of my head. I sat down in front of the computer at my desk and I said, "I gotta do this. I gotta get her off my back." I had never used eBay before, but I typed in the eBay URL, registered an account, and— Call the cops! This has got to be illegal! Two minutes left and some guy named bodyshop44 just put an $1,800 bid on my pool table! Never in my wildest dreams did I think this would happen. Just one more refresh— Doh! brucelightning just outbid bodyshop44, and it's up to $1,825. Come on, bodyshop44, this baby is yours! You need my pool table!

My goodness, I've got to calm down or I'll wake my fiancée up. My story's almost done here. I created my account, and even though I'd never used eBay before, I scanned in some stock photos I had from the store and I listed this pool table on eBay. And then I prayed for the last three days that no one would buy it.

OK, I can't take it anymore. I've got to refresh again. F5. F5! There's one minute to go and, wait, who is this? spicyinmiami thinks she can prance right in and outbid brucelightning. And what about bodyshop44?? This pool table is his! But not if you're gonna give me $2,000 for it! Goodbye bodyshop44, hello spicyinmiami.

F5. Ah, brucelightning is back with a vengeance. $2,025 strong. Not so spicy in Miami anymore, is it?

F5. What? Who are you? You're going to bid *how much?* You're my new best friend, burleetrucker!

F5. Fifteen seconds. spicyinmiami just ran my trucker friend off the road. $2,100.

F5. $2,125, and it's brucelightning in the lead with twelve seconds to go.

F5. $2,175. I'm feeling queasy. "Honey, you've got to see this!"

F5. $2,225. Four seconds left, and my new best friend the trucker is on the road again! Looks like this baby's all yours!

F5. Auction ended. $2,250. Winning bidder—I don't believe it, it's bodyshop44! I knew it was yours all along, buddy! I swear I never doubted you once.

Oh my God. I think I just sold a pool table on eBay.

True story.

Why eBay?

There are a million reasons to start selling on eBay. Perhaps your aunt gave you a plastic lawn gnome for Christmas and it's the ugliest thing you've ever seen, but you notice that someone's selling one just like it on eBay and you figure why not sell yours, too. Maybe you collect Pan Am Airlines memorabilia and you know it would be the perfect place to sell your extra pair of Pan Am in-flight booties and perhaps find that "Gone, But Not Forgotten" license plate frame you saw on I-95 last week. You might be looking for a way to make a few extra bucks on the side to pay for your newly upgraded Premium Cable TV status, because your wife has been depressed ever since she missed the entire season of Ralphie on *The Sopranos* after you refused to get HBO.

Yes, there are millions of reasons to start selling on eBay. You might be in the market for a part-time job to make ends meet when your day job, or night job, just isn't cutting it. Perhaps you are sick and tired of hearing the same "it's just not feasible right now, but we'll see in six months" excuse for denying you a raise from a boss who's been driving a limited-edition Jaguar XK-R to the office every morning since he sold the Porsche. Maybe you were the latest victim of "cost-cutting" at your firm, and you know there has to be a better solution to your situation than staring at Monster.com watching how many hits your résumé is getting and wondering if you're going to get hired before the paltry checks stop coming in from the unemployment office.

Perhaps you're doing just fine, but you know you could be getting more out of life and you're ready to take charge of your career. Perhaps you're ready to join the ranks of 150,000 others by using the eBay marketplace to build a serious and rewarding full-time business, or the more than 450,000 who use eBay to provide a supplemental part-time income. Or, by chance, like me, you might just want to get your mom off your back.

There are big differences in these approaches to eBay, and, more important, big differences in the results you'll get based on the approach you take. If you are one of the majority of eBay users who are happy to keep their eBay experience as a hobby or sporadic transactional venture, then there is really no need to change anything at all in your approach to eBay. You are getting what you need and what you want out of it, and are, in large part, the foundation of eBay's marketplace.

My guess is, however, that if you picked up this book in the first place, you're hoping to get more out of eBay than just a purchase or a sale here and there. You might not have any experience in business, or with the Internet, but you have a PowerSeller star in your eye. The good news is you're on the right track. The bad news is it's going to take some effort on your part. The good news about the bad news is it's easier than you may think. If your goal is to achieve a consistent part-time income from eBay, or to join the ranks of those 150,000 people making a successful full-time living with eBay, then you have a lot to gain by reading this book.

eBay's Here to Stay

It is becoming clear to economic experts and laypeople alike that the eBay juggernaut is on an unmistakable path. That path is creating great successes in its wake. In an economy that experts say is not so great, eBay increased its earnings 92 percent from the first quarter in 2003 to the first quarter in 2004. As of this writing, eBay's stock is at an all-time high. Meg Whitman, eBay's CEO, predicted in 2003 that eBay would be doing $3 billion in sales by 2005. By January 2004, she announced that they would be hitting that mark a year ahead of schedule. Four months later, in May 2004, they had revised the estimate upwards to $3.2 billion. A $200 million increase in earnings projections in less than a third of a year is an exciting prospect for anyone, let alone anyone with a vested interest in eBay's success. But that's not nearly the whole of it.

More important to you and me:

Fun Fact

There were $28 billion in transactional dollars spent on eBay in 2004.

That's a lot of household caddy baskets, not to mention larger than many countries' GDPs. There were 80 million members on eBay in 2003. By the fourth quarter of 2004, there were over 115 million registered members on track to significantly outdo 2003's numbers. The question is, how much of that $24 billion and counting do you want? It would be great to have a billion of it, but it would be good to have a couple thousand of it as well. For every transaction on eBay, there is a buyer and a seller, and if you are a seller, there is a piece of that $24 billion pie that is waiting to be sent directly to your PayPal account. Perhaps a substantial piece, enough to give you the financial freedom you are seeking.

I haven't yet found a crystal ball on eBay that actually works, although I haven't won any auctions for those, either. Nonetheless, I have been a student of business my entire life, and the signs are crystal clear. eBay will continue to grow at a fantastic rate for years to come. The good news for you is that

Quick Tip

The greatest success stories on eBay have yet to be written.

Given the phenomenal success of eBay to date, that is an unquestionably bold statement to make.

Yet one must look no further than the power of networks and the power of community to come to the same conclusion. eBay's growth has been driven primarily by word of mouth, still the best form of advertisement. As the time-worn adage in sales goes:

Quick Tip

"The more you sell, the more you sell."

This applies doubly to the eBay community, because it is based both on sellers and buyers. The more people use eBay, the more people tell others about it. The more products are sold on eBay, the more customers will buy on eBay. And the more buyers there are on eBay, the more sellers there will be. It is an ever-widening globe-crossing circle of influence. The number of members keeps increasing because an increasing number of members are promoting it every day. This growth might lead one to say, "eBay isn't what it used to be." Indeed, it's not. It gets better every year. Back in 1995, eBay founder Pierre Omidyar envisioned a new era of financial empowerment that would arise with the advent of a truly democratic marketplace accessible to people of all walks of life. This is the reality of eBay today.

When you consider what the marketplace on eBay has to offer, it becomes clear that we are still early in the curve. Even the cream of the crop on eBay, the three hundred or so Titanium PowerSellers who are averaging *at least* $150,000 in gross sales every month, are still learning. After all, it's easy to forget that this phenomenon we call eBay is merely a few years old. Most businesses don't

New people joining in now and launching new businesses can piggyback on the experience of guys like me. They can learn from our mistakes and from our successes, and they can slingshot into the future.

hit full stride until they're at least ten years old or older. Microsoft was a tiny company at ten years old, a small fraction of what eBay is today. Human nature being what it is, the eBay marketplace will continue to improve, innovate, and expand.

Cracking the Code

When I began to organize my thoughts on my eBay experience and put together my "Fast Cash" guide for eBay success, I purchased and read every book I could find about eBay, and I noticed a consistent theme. Almost without exception, each one explained how to get started either buying or selling on eBay, but the chapters that focused on selling were very basic in nature. Most of the information, in fact, was already contained in eBay's online educational tutorials. The textbook guides are out there, and some are quite good. However, in my research, I was unable to find a book written by a *top-seller* who had actually started from scratch on eBay and built a thriving business. There was nothing for a reader in the form of specific detailed techniques and insights on how to grow a business on eBay.

I have been approached countless times over the past few years with the same question asked in just so many ways:

"Can you teach me how to get started on eBay, and then can you teach me to become really successful?"

It's become clear to me that there are a growing number of people who want help to get them to the point of making substantial profits on eBay. They want to know how to make money consistently using the eBay market-place. What started out as a passing thought for me— "How can I answer this question without sharing my own experience?"—has evolved into a detailed and in-depth guide for anyone who would like to start their own eBay business and become their own eBay success story. In this book, I will take you along on my journey to financial success through eBay. It is my own personal journey to enlightenment.

I will show you how I went from trying to prove my mother wrong to simply being intrigued by selling on eBay, to becoming owner and operator of a multimillion-dollar corporation.

I wish I'd had someone to learn from when I began on eBay. It would have saved me a tremendous amount of time, heartache, and money. But I consider myself a first-generation PowerSeller and an eBay education specialist, which reflects not only my success but my desire to share that success with others. You can do more on eBay than I've done, and in less time than I've done it, because I'm laying the blueprint out for you in sharing what I've learned.

You will be able to propel your business further into the future than I did when I started, because you'll have a roadmap and a set of tools along with it that I never had.

As I've worked with others and shared these concepts with them, I discovered that the knowledge I shared not only worked—but worked well. Real people with absolutely no online selling experience have applied these strategies and techniques and achieved dramatic results. It was the realization that this information can be utilized by virtually anyone that solidified the concept and my conviction in actually documenting these techniques. You can take the techniques and become a PowerSeller on eBay.

I achieved PowerSeller status on eBay in a manner that can—and will—be replicated over and over again by the next generation of PowerSeller—*you*. You've made the first move by picking up this book. Now it's time to crack the code, so let's begin.

Part One

INTRODUCTION

Live the Dream

eBay Tonight

When I started selling on eBay, I would have loved to sit down with somebody and have that person teach me everything. I wanted the whole package, all the systems. I wanted to know what to say and I wanted to know what to do. I found some good books, some interesting reading material spread around the Web, and some great tutorials provided by eBay itself. There was nothing, however, that said to me, "here's a proven model for success."

You can walk into any McDonald's anywhere, and it will look and feel just about the same as any other McDonald's. All the Big Macs taste the same, all the Chicken McNuggets taste the same, it all looks and smells the same, and each and every store has a consistent stream of hungry consumers walking in and out every day. It is the ultimate example of the franchise concept. It's a proven business model. When you open a McDonald's franchise, you step onto a moving platform, a ready-to-go business system that tells you, step-by-step, how it works. If you follow it, you will be successful.

Quick Tip

What I've outlined in this book is a proven business model that, at one point, yielded my eBay stores close to a million dollars a month in real, tangible sales on eBay.

This book is peppered with insider strategies and tips that are based on my real experiences on eBay. It's not necessary to go through the long and steep learning curve that I've gone through. Of course, we'll all make some mistakes along the way, but the more we can shortcut those mistakes, the more assured we are of success. I learned the hard way, but I was also lucky enough to come to eBay from a successful career in business. I've had experience helping both seasoned businesspeople and total newbies to the business world. Likewise, I've helped people with no Internet experience whatsoever both expand their current brick-and-mortar business to the

Quick Tip

It works. Anyone can do it—and *you* can do it, too!

eBay platform and start entirely new businesses. Here's what I've learned from all of this advising:

How I Got Here in the First Place

The first real job I ever had was selling kitchen knives for a direct-sales company during my senior year at Tulane in New Orleans. It was an in-home sales job, which meant I had to start out selling to my family and friends. My family is in New York, and my friends weren't ready to buy kitchen knives yet, so I had to figure out another way to get started. I began selling to my professors, and they eventually led me to their friends, acquaintances, and family, and so on, for several degrees of separation. They were good knives and they had a lifetime warranty, so you could put them in the dishwasher and dig holes in the backyard with them if you wanted. With the lifetime warranty, all you had to do was send in your old ones and the company would replace them, at any time, for as long as you live. Before the year was over, I could count nearly the entire New Orleans Saints squad on my roster. I had become the number-one sales rep in a company of thirty thousand.

Over that summer, I decided to skip my law school plans and join the company full-time as a manager. Ten years and thousands of paring knives later, during the height of the tech boom in the summer of 1999, I left direct sales and moved to San Diego to work for an Internet start-up. If you're at all familiar with the history of the Internet, and the fate of most online businesses, then you probably already know the eventual outcome of the path that I was now embarking on.

Quick Tip

That crystal ball *I didn't have* would certainly have come in handy.

I worked for almost two years, day and night, for almost no pay. Luckily for me, I did receive a healthy share of stock options. I was caught up in the stock market Internet craze and I actually had begun counting down the days until the IPO and the future valuation of my stock options. I was rich—in my head. I was making plans about where to live, what cars to buy, and which vacations I would take first. I could remember staying up late with friends fantasizing about what it would be like to have millions and millions of dollars.

The company into which I had put so much dedication, hard work, and effort finally filed for its long-awaited IPO in March 2000. The company had waited and waited and waited until the time was finally right to go public. The road show was over. The funds were raised. The investment banking company gave us the go-ahead with a strong approval rating. And then—can you fill in the rest? The market crashed. The Internet bubble burst, and the IPO never happened. The company filed for bankruptcy, was sold for pennies on the dollar, and my stock options, hundreds of thousands of them, burned gloriously in my ersatz fireplace.

I was at a crossroads in my life, faced with an uncomfortable situation and a difficult decision to make. Where do I go from here? How do I pick up the pieces and start over? I had lived the last two years basically on my savings, since my income at the start-up was significantly less than the market value for the position I held. This was my own choice, of course, with the remainder of my compensation being in instantly worthless stock options. At the age of thirty-three, I found myself out of work, $80,000 in debt, and down about $300,000 as a result of the crash of the stock market, not counting the millions the stock would have been worth. Although my situation was all but unique, there was no doubt that I was in the wrong place at the wrong time.

I started to look for work in the newspaper. Of course, with countless thousands of Internet refugees in the same position I was in, the job market was tight. I prepared a résumé and went on some interviews, but my heart really wasn't in it. I was accustomed to making a comfortable living, and the best job I could find offered me 60 percent of what I needed to earn to pay down my debt. That just wasn't going to cut it for me.

During this time, I got a phone call from a former colleague who said he wanted me to listen to an audio recording about a new home-based business opportunity that he thought would be perfect for me. I had heard some horror stories in the past, regarding sham home-based business solutions, so I was reluctant to give even an hour of my time to the tapes. However, I happened to trust this person, and I decided to go against my instinct and have a listen. It took about a half hour and, I have to admit, it was exciting. I was motivated after I heard the tapes, and I went ahead and wrote a check for $495, sent it off in the mail, and about a week later, I received a kit full of manuals, books, and more tapes.

The basis of the program was that I needed to call people I knew, get them to listen to the recording, and then sell the books and tapes to them.

As you can imagine, it wasn't long before I became very uncomfortable with the entire program. Any program that was based on me selling to my friends and family, who then sold to their friends and family, and so on and so forth, with no real value added in the entire process, disturbed me implicitly.

Still, the concept of having a home-based business was intriguing to me, so I did some research. I read magazine articles and newspaper ads, and I browsed the Internet and discovered that most of these business opportunities were focused on getting rich quick.

The more I read, the more I realized that the vast majority of these opportunities were unrealistic and impossible to attain.

There may be one or two people out there who gain the promised results of a successful home-based income, but for the average person like me, there was no real way of ever achieving those goals through those programs.

I decided soon after that experience that I would go into business for myself and, not being able to come up with any other alternatives at the time, I ended up opening a small retail furniture store. I sold all types of furniture for the home and then expanded my product line to include pool tables and spas. Business was good, but running the store all by myself took a toll on me. I hated being at the store all day. I am not a creature of schedule, and sticking to the same store hours every week was not my cup of tea. I have never been a nine-to-fiver, but I needed the steady income, so I stuck it out for the time being. And then I discovered eBay.

I sold my first pool table on eBay after my mother insisted I give it a try. To my utter surprise, not only did I sell that first pool table, I sold it for $300 more than it went for at my store. More successful pool-table auctions followed, and I was thrilled. I phoned my mother and relinquished my pride. She'd been right all along about eBay.

"What did I tell you, Adam?"

If I could write the next version of Robert Kiyosaki's book *Rich Dad, Poor Dad,* and title it *Insistent Mom, Right Mom,* then lesson number one would have to be "Listen to your mother."

That was October 2001. It was November 2002 before I took eBay seriously. I didn't know anything about it. I didn't even know what a PowerSeller was. I knew that I had developed a neat sales channel on the side to rid myself of some extra billiard inventory, that it was easy enough to do, and that it was fun. That's about all I cared about. I had gone through the period in January 2002 when all of my listings were coming down.

In February, I had conversed with an eBay attorney who happened to have bid on one of my pool tables and who'd offered to help. In March, I had worked with a gentleman from Policies and Procedures, whom the lawyer had put me in touch with, and we had run through every possible policy issue to make sure that I didn't get any more auctions closed down. Despite all this attention, I still had no idea what I was dealing with. I had no idea that I was quickly becoming one of their top sellers and they had taken notice.

In April, I got a call from someone at eBay asking me if I wanted to participate in a program called eBay Voices. eBay Voices is a two-day forum the company puts together every two months, to meet with several dozen people from all walks of the eBay community, from the most advanced to the most basic sellers, and pick their brains for the issues that concern them and ideas they have to make eBay better. I agreed to join and, as quickly as I hung up the phone, realized that I was getting married that weekend in June, so I called back and turned it down. They called me two months later and invited me to the forum in August, but it just so happened that the date coincided with my honeymoon, so I had to turn the invitation down again.

Lucky for me, they didn't give up, and I was invited again, this time for the November forum. I flew up to San Jose and took a taxi to their campus. I was amazed by the sheer grandeur of it all, as if I was walking through an Ivy League campus minus the bad weather. Inside their offices, the prominent feeling you got was one of openness, from the layout of the cubicles to the casual dress of the employees. I soon learned that eBay counted four thousand–plus employees among its workforce, and that fact, together with how impressed I was by their facility, made me realize that this was a very big deal, far bigger than I had ever imagined.

Quick Tip

With big deals come big opportunities, and it hit me that I had this vast opportunity right in front of me. That's when I said, "OK, that's it, it's eBay from here on out." It was my moment of truth.

In the week that followed my visit to San Jose, I closed the furniture shop. The course had been set, and I was riding full-steam-ahead.

The eBay Revolution

These days, it's hard to escape news of the exciting things that are happening on eBay. Any article written about the success of Internet commerce in recent years cannot be complete without a mention of the amazing role of online auctions in this success. Undoubtedly, eBay is setting the precedent for the rest of the pack. eBay is one of the world's fastest-growing enterprises. How often has someone said to you, "I got that on eBay; I couldn't find it anywhere else," or, "You know what? You should sell that on eBay." As big as it is, it is still gathering steam, an unstoppable force redesigning the modern economic landscape like a category-five hurricane.

eBay is perhaps the phenomenon of the century. It is a revolution, representing an entirely new business model. It is one of those applications that constantly remind us what profound societal and economic implications the Internet has. When Al Gore invented the Internet, I'm sure eBay was what he had in mind. eBay fulfills the promise of the Internet Age by connecting buyers and sellers inexpensively and almost effortlessly. It has created its own community, marketplace, nomenclature, protocol, and even its own constellation of stars— the PowerSellers.

 Quick Tip

eBay is a great democratizer. It presents a level playing field, allowing the most inexperienced seller to compete with multibillion-dollar conglomerates. On eBay, they are equals.

It puts power into the hands of those who have never tasted it, offering them financial freedom and the ability to live out their dreams. The founder of eBay, Pierre Omidyar, wrote the code for the Web site in his basement, dreaming of a virtual trading post where anyone could conduct business from anywhere, on an equal basis. He dreamed big, but the results of that dream are even bigger. Pierre himself could not have imagined the worldwide powerhouse his little experiment would become.

eBay is a selling platform unparalleled in the history of man. It has more than 42,000 different product categories.

Fun Fact

There are 79 million searches and 7.7 million bids placed every day. Sellers on eBay gross 50 million dollars combined every single day.

Is it any wonder that more and more large corporations are viewing eBay as a necessary addition to their selling arena? Companies like Motorola, BMW, and the Sharper Image are all getting on the bandwagon. Why? Because eBay works—big-time. With all of this, the small entrepreneurs can readily and effectively compete with the big guys, because the playing field is level. Everyone is treated equally, and the rules are the same for everyone. It used to be that big companies squashed small companies all across America. How many local drugstores have been driven out of business by CVS? In the restaurant business, even the auto-repair business, the big guys have a significant advantage because of economies of scale. But eBay has changed all that. eBay is an equalizer. It brings the big boys down to our size—or maybe, I should say, gives us the tools to effectively compete with them on their level.

eBay provides a fundamental shift in the modern con-
sumer's life. We are no longer helpless consumers
enslaved by the economic system of our culture. We now
have a way to seize the system and make it work for us.
On eBay, the sky is the limit with regard to earning poten-
tial. All you need are good resources, the right business
system, and the drive to make it happen. You'll be
amazed by how quickly and easily your business will turn
a profit.

The genius of eBay is the freedom it can provide. You can escape the bureaucracy of a nine-to-five job. You will set your own schedule, answering to no one. There are no limits. You can do as much or as little as you decide. You can make eBay a part-time venture that helps add to your bottom line with a little profit and a lot of tax benefits, or you can jump in the deep end right away, starting a new life with your eBay User ID.

I write this book with a purpose—to provide you with the instructional insight necessary for you to thrive and prosper on eBay. By understanding and implementing the business principles and techniques necessary to succeed on the site, you are choosing to remove yourself from the confines of a limited society. Building a successful eBay business can and will provide you with the money and, even more important, with the time you crave to go off and enjoy life.

On eBay, the entrepreneurial spirit of the American dream
becomes the reality of a worldwide opportunity.

eBay provides you with the opportunity to excel, to do something professional you've never done before, and to enjoy true independence. You can perform at your own pace as you strive to achieve your goals. If you are serious about taking control of your future, it is time to begin or further your eBay success.

If you've ever considered opening your own business, you'll know that just the thought process involved in counting the list of essentials can be daunting. You need a physical location for your customers to come to when they want to do business with you. You need a staff of employees, a warehouse filled with inventory, an advertising budget. Back in business school, I came across something the great department-store pioneer J. C. Penney once said: "I know that only 50 percent of my advertising is effective, and 50 percent is wasted. I just don't know which 50 percent is which." An advertising campaign is an educated guess at best. Even a small display ad in the local newspaper can cost hundreds of dollars. Radio will cost you thousands, and television and magazine ads upwards of tens of thousands of dollars.

Well, you can throw all this out the window with eBay.

Quick Tip

On eBay, you have instant access to 115 million customers and counting without spending a dime on advertising. eBay brings the buyers to you. One thing's for sure: they didn't teach me that at business school.

You can now work from the comfort of your home, taking advantage of the greatest home-based business opportunity ever. You can operate from your den with no additional rent expense whatsoever. In fact, you'll make money, because you'll now be able to deduct a portion of your home. All you need is a computer, Internet access, and a phone. This book will help you on your way, as well.

The general public does not yet realize the amazing potential eBay holds. Over 175,000 people use eBay as their full-time income, which is remarkable, considering the site is not yet a decade old. eBay has more than 115 million members and more sign on every single day. My eBay watch store has sold watches to customers in over forty countries. eBay is not only fulfilling the promise of the American dream, but the global one. eBay exists as a gateway to freedom wherever a computer has access to the Internet. Craftswomen in small villages have used it to sell their wares to buyers halfway around the world and improve their quality of life. eBay itself has set up native sites in twenty-two countries with a commitment to continue its international expansion.

When I opened up my brick-and-mortar furniture store, an excessively busy day would see maybe twelve to fifteen customers. I used to sell about four or five pool tables in a good week. When I signed on to eBay, I had immediate access to its millions and millions of members. As soon as you click on the "Ship Worldwide" on your listing page, you are running an international company. You may be operating out of your garage, but your computer places your business smack in the middle of a multifaceted global marketplace, by far the largest of its kind.

eBay even has its own currency that is accepted every-where in the world, further evidence that the Web site is a true tool for market globalization. The predominant method for payment on eBay is PayPal.

eBay is an extraordinary system—easy, secure, and ubiquitous. You no longer have to acquire a merchant account to accept credit cards. You can sign up for PayPal and immediately anyone anywhere can pay you with any major credit card or actual money they have sitting in their bank account. They do all international currency conversions automatically. You won't even know your customer paid in yen. I recently left feedback for an international buyer. I checked out their other feedback and couldn't read most of it, because it was all in different languages. The Planet Earth is now your showroom.

Live the Dream

Words of Wisdom

"Better to light a candle than curse the darkness."
—*Chinese proverb*

I hated my store. I hated the schedule, I hated having to get up every morning at a certain time and I hated being stuck there all day long every day of the week. I hated the smell. I began to hate even the street it was on.

If I wasn't headed there for some reason, I would avoid that street at all costs. People go into business for themselves thinking they'll have more time for themselves. I found out the hard way that the opposite is usually true. You end up working a lot harder a lot more hours for yourself, trying to get your business up and profitable. You think, going in, that this is your key to freedom, and it ends up being your key to killing yourself. You become a slave to it.

eBay was the answer to all my problems, challenges, and frustrations.

My eBay business has gotten huge, but I still run it as opposed to it running me. I come and go as I please, my daughter remembers what I look like now, and my wife doesn't feel the need to put out a missing person's ad.

My family no longer has to search for me on the back of milk cartons. We went on a cruise to the Mediterranean. I brought my laptop and was able to run my business from France, Spain, and Greece. You can go anywhere and do anything and still be connected to your business. I probably shouldn't have been working at all on vacation, as my wife repeatedly told me, but I did it because I wanted to—because eBay is fun—and not because I had to. eBay is wherever you want it to be.

While running a seminar in San Francisco recently, I met a pleasant couple who were self-proclaimed "hippie-gypsies." They told me they wanted to start an eBay business because they didn't want "to work nine to five and punch a time clock and be slave to somebody else's dream." They had met another couple in Arizona, who made their living selling on eBay while traveling around on a bus they had converted to accommodate their business. Now they wanted to do the same thing. They were inspired by others who were using eBay to support "the hippie-gypsy way," as they called it. They came to my seminar because they had glimpsed the possible and wanted to make that dream come true for themselves.

eBay can help you make your dreams come true no matter what they are. You may dream about driving around the country in a Volkswagen van leaving peace and love in your wake. You may harbor a secret desire of becoming a world championship juggler but can't currently afford the time required to practice your craft. You may want to retire, creating time to visit your kids and hang out on the beach. You may just want a little extra income to help you get out of debt and maybe fund a family vacation to the Grand Canyon. Everyone has a dream. No matter what yours is, eBay can help you realize it.

Words of Wisdom

"Believe in yourself! Have faith in your abilities! Without a humble but reasonable confidence in your own powers you cannot be successful or happy." —*Norman Vincent Peale*

eBay Taps into Human Nature

My mother is the perfect example of a model eBayer. On the wall next to her computer, she has a bulletin board. This bulletin board is overflowing with photographs of the people she has befriended on eBay. They come to do business, but they leave as friends. A year or so ago, she received an e-mail from a gentleman whose wife had just given birth to a premature little girl. She weighed one pound and was only barely grasping on to life. The situation was a moment-to-moment hell for her parents. The father actually took time away from his vigil to e-mail my mother with a list of one hundred and ten Beanie Babies they wanted for the little girl's nursery. I suppose it was the only productive thing he felt he could do in the long hours of waiting. Touched, my mother bundled up the Beanie Babies on his list and sent them off without asking for or agreeing to accept payment. The little girl survived her battle, and her father and my mother still carry on a close e-mail and Instant Message relationship. eBay is anything but anonymous.

An interesting phenomenon of the Internet Age is that it has revived certain aspects of society that were all but lost ten or twenty years ago. It is frequently mentioned that e-mail has brought back the art of letter-writing, an art that, if not dead, was definitely being handed its hat. eBay, with its strong sense of community, has returned us to the days of the town market, where people went to shop and be social, to catch up on the news of the day and say hello to their friends.

---

eBay is fun.

That's one of the key reasons for its success. More than simply a marketplace that brings together buyers and sellers, eBay is a marketplace community that people want to shop at. There are two main components of the eBay fun factor. The first is the sense of community, grown from a seedling in the early days of the site to a full-blown forest today. People are not anonymous on eBay. There are 115 million and counting individuals on the site, and each matters equally. Members interact. Friendships are formed. Every day, people cruise the discussion boards where familiar names and voices can be found all the time. eBay itself fostered this environment, involving the community in important business decisions since the very beginning. Any time they failed to include the community, they heard about it in spades and were forced to remember why the site had been started in the first place.

Until recently, eBay did not advertise. People found it by happenstance or word of mouth, and felt as if it was their own discovery. It was a special place, where people trusted one another and formed bonds that reached beyond a few transactions. eBay started as a small grassroots community, and, by population, it would currently be the eleventh largest nation in the world, about equal in size to Mexico. It still, however, has retained its strong human ties. eBay is a place where you can go and find friends among the people you do business with.

Selling on eBay is different.

It's counterculture: to run a business on the Internet, where consumers can't actually touch and feel what they're buying. It's a community based on trust, where a buyer is willing to pay for an item from a seller they have not met, for an item they have not seen, and trust that the seller will ship the item as described. It's a community where the seller relies on the integrity of the buyer to pay for the merchandise that they've purchased. It's a marketplace where sellers can provide goods and service without the overhead and inventory requirements of a typical brick-and-mortar store. Buying and selling online is a unique experience. It goes against the flow, like rowing upstream. Many of the basic principles of retail apply online, yet the mindset is different. Conventional wisdom tells us that people want to see what they're buying before they buy it. But in the world today, buying online is becoming more common than ever. And where there are buyers, there must be sellers.

In addition to the sense of community you can find on eBay, there is also great excitement.

Quick Tip

Auctions are adrenaline-pumping, heart-racing, thrilling affairs.

If you've never used eBay before, you'll become very familiar with one important button on your keyboard.

The F5 key refreshes the screen. Imagine you've found that rare beer stein you've been hunting for for decades on eBay. You're the high bidder and there are three minutes left in the auction. Someone outbids you and the battle is on. The F5 key becomes your best friend. It is there for you as a buyer and it is there for you as a seller. When a bidding war rages for one of your items, you'll love it as much as I do.

Fun Fact

eBay has officially been declared an addiction.

Experts have outlined the four signs that you suffer from an eBay addiction. First is that you spend more than two hours a day, five days a week, logged on to auctions as a buyer. If you're a seller, you may be on the site a lot more than that. Second is that you bid for things on the site you'd never buy in an actual store. Third is that you set an alarm for the end of auctions regardless of the time, day or night. Finally, you are obsessed with the eBay lingo and etiquette. If you are a buyer, I might recommend getting help, but if you are a seller, a very mild addiction can only help your business. Imagine if you were addicted to your current employment.

eBay is addicting because it is fun. It is similar to the experience of gambling in a casino. It is a game. My wife and my mother are in it for the pure fun. It's not about the money for them. It's about the fun of the bidding, the fun of the sniping, the fun of the selling, the pleasure experience when someone actually buys one of their items. If you ask my mother how she feels about eBay, she can't answer without using the word "love" at least four times.

"I love it, I love it, I love it, I love it,"is her typical response.

For twelve years, she and my father went to Atlantic City every weekend. Now she has eBay. This juggernaut isn't going anywhere, because people love it. A strong international marketplace mixed with a healthy dose of community and a dash of adrenaline and excitement is a recipe that will not fail.

A Replicable System

I had been running my pool table business for about eighteen months when I had a brainstorm. Maybe I could generate the same success for other products as we had for pool tables. I called my father-in-law. He's been in the watch-and-jewelry business for thirty-five years. He has a retail store and he wants to retire. I said, "Howard, why don't we work together and try selling some of your watches on eBay?" His reaction was similar to the one I had when my mother started in on me. He didn't own a computer and had never used the Internet. As a matter of fact, he had never even sent an e-mail. To this day, he continues to learn. He was impressed by my success, however, and was willing to give it a try. He now knows how to check his listings and see who's paid and who hasn't. After a year, he may understand only the very basics of how to use the computer, but he has a strong grasp on the principles required for success on eBay. My little experiment worked.

Howard is now one of the top watch sellers on eBay and a top seller of both Seiko and Citizen watches in the United States.

These days I'm barely involved in his business. I simply taught my father-in-law the same principles and techniques we employed to sell our pool tables. He now sells more watches in a week than he ever did in a year in his bricks-and-mortar store.

After the watch experiment worked, I began branching out into other products. I now have a variety of eBay stores, selling everything from diamonds to spas, scooters to tanning beds. I have not succeeded with every single product that I tried, but it is inexpensive to experiment on eBay, and when I encountered a product that didn't work, I would quickly move on.

The reality is that it does not matter what you are selling. Some people want to sell products they really like. I learned a long time ago that it's not really necessary to like what you are selling—you're not selling to yourself. The key is to sell what people are willing to buy.

Pool tables are, in fact, one of the harder items to sell, because of their size. The information herein is generic and it works. Lift out one product and replace it with another. We've cracked the eBay code so that you can sell virtually anything and find success.

What You Will Learn

We have all been taught to get a good job with a good company, work hard and do our best to claw our way up through the system. As I have been saying, eBay offers a way to shortcut that. Business schools around the country teach a traditional model for starting a business. It looks something like this:

- You will end your first year of operations in debt.
- In the second year, you will perhaps break even.
- If you are lucky, you will finally turn a profit your third year in business.

eBay has turned this traditional model on its ear.

Quick Tip

If you list your first auction tonight, your business can be profitable three days from now.

eBay is about taking action. This is a groundbreaking concept. It is possible because of the incredibly low start-up costs and overhead required to build and run an eBay business.

In this book, I will not tell you exactly what to do at each and every stage. What works for one product may not work for another. As well, eBay continues to change—and that is why I offer ongoing support to those looking for information on the latest, greatest secrets to success on eBay. I will, however, provide a way of thinking, a system of strategies and techniques you can use as the foundation of your eBay enterprise. I don't know if you ever had a Rubik's cube, but I did. It drove me crazy. I tried to figure the damn thing out for months and finally I just took the stickers off and rearranged them so I could make it look like it was supposed to. A friend of my parents saw what I had done and gave me a cheat-sheet instruction manual. After that, I could solve that Rubik's cube in under an hour. Your time is valuable—don't spend two years making mistakes, as I did. Use this book as your cheat-sheet instruction manual, and you won't have to.

- This book is a model for future successes.
- You'll learn what eBay is and how you can use it best to sell more.
- You'll learn the eBay marketplace, what types of products to sell, and how to obtain them.
- You'll learn how to set up your home office and operate your own accounting system effectively.
- You'll learn to create high-quality photographs of your products guaranteed to increase your sales.

- You'll learn listing strategies and promotions.
- You'll learn the importance of eBay feedback: it can make or break you.
- You'll discover actions for post-auction follow-up.
- You'll learn how your eBay venture can save you thousands of dollars in personal taxes, and everything else you need to know to run a powerful eBay business.

eBay Tonight

You can put this book down and begin realizing your dreams tonight. Even if you've never signed on to eBay, you can begin instantaneously.

Quick Tip

No matter what level you're at, you can use these strategies tonight.

You can buy first, to learn the ins and outs of the Web site and build your feedback. You can list your first item, and your global operation will be open for business tonight. If you're already selling, you can use these tips and techniques to improve your existing business and increase your profitability.

Take action. eBay is sitting there waiting for you.

I want to encourage you to find your eBay moment of truth, when you realize the possibilities out there. It took almost a year before I found mine and began taking eBay seriously. I was slow. It shouldn't have taken me that long. Start tonight, and your revelation is just around the corner.

CHAPTER TWO

Thinking Like an Entrepreneur

"Adam, I really hope you know what you're doing." I hadn't seen Jennifer look this serious since one of her patients broke out of the hospital and took four hostages to a paintball range.

"I think I'm serious. I really do." I had no idea if it could work, but that was the most truthful answer I could give her. The fact was, anything looked better than the status quo. I couldn't spend another day at the store without knowing this episode of my life would quickly be coming to a close. Could this eBay thing really work out? It sure seemed like it could. Would it last? Was the bubble just slow to burst for this one Internet site, or were its fundamentals actually strong enough to make it immune to market volatility?

These were questions I was willing to have unanswered for the time being. I was confident enough in my sales figures for the last six months on eBay, and I was even more confident in the knowledge that this store was quite literally sucking me dry of any hope I was able to muster after my firm went belly-up. Cautiously, I took Jennifer aside and told her to keep this to herself until I was certain about what I was doing. She was all too happy to oblige.

Monday morning, at 8:30 a.m., I had begun the phone calls to de-brick-and-mortarize my life, and by Thursday afternoon I was the proud un-owner of a retail store on the corner of Overland and Venice in Los Angeles. The other shoe had dropped on the fat lady's foot and she promptly had begun to sing. I was a free man—free to take my eBay business to the next level.

Every one of the hundreds of thousands of folks who are buying and selling on eBay and making money in the process has a story of how they began on the site and when they began to take it seriously. As people begin to read and hear about the success stories of others, the "curve to seriousness" on eBay becomes shorter and shorter.

When I started, I hadn't heard of anyone making a substantial primary income from eBay. Frankly, I had never thought about it, even as I was pulling in the sales figures that should have been like neon signs to me. Call me slow to the punch. Meanwhile, somebody starting today might already have an idea about the serious income potential available to them on eBay. If you're reading this book, I'm going to bet that you've thought about it at least once or twice. What it means for you is that right from the very beginning, you're going to have your head in the right place, and that place is in thinking like an entrepreneur.

Words of Wisdom

"There is only one way to make a great deal of money; and that is in a business of your own."
—*J. Paul Getty*

This is the absolute first step to starting an eBay business. If you haven't done so already,

adjust your approach to eBay and take the entrepreneurial point of view.

You need to think like a business owner in order to realize the potential of eBay. Once you have the entrepreneurial mindset, it is only a matter of time before you will seize that potential. The whole question of "is this a business or a hobby?" really begins in the eye of the beholder. The answer is all in the approach. How are you going to structure this? Most people get started selling on eBay by unloading their old antiques, outdated electronics, clothes that don't fit anymore, and other assorted junk in and around the house. When their online garage sale is a smashing success, it dawns on them that there may be something to this eBay thing. They think, "I can make this into a full-time business." They search for inventory, experiment with listing strategies, and begin putting the systems into place to run a legitimate business.

The entrepreneurial point of view is a mentality. Whether you plan to work part-time a few hours a week while still maintaining your current employment or drop everything to give eBay 100 percent of your attention, you are still starting a business. Since you have a business, think like a businessperson. My mentor, a brilliant businessman and leader, Don Freda, taught me a useful business proverb known universally as the "as if" principle:

Quick Tip

If you think and act "as if" you are running a successful business, you will be.

Assume the position and it will assume you. Your eBay business has the potential to become a profit-making steamroller, turning you into a millionaire in the process. Your enterprise is a serious thing and deserves a serious commitment.

eBay may be the largest and most advanced flea market in the world, but it is so much more than that. As a business opportunity, it is unrivaled. Never before has a seller had access to 115 million customers and counting at the click of a button.

To say that you can be in business globally for thirty cents tonight is unheard of.

eBay can work for you even if you have no business experience whatsoever. In fact, it is the perfect arena for someone starting out because the start-up costs and overhead are incredibly low. You can gain your business experience for pennies on the dollar of what a brick-and-mortar retail store would cost you.

Owning your own business and achieving financial freedom has always been the American dream.

Historically, most people have been unable to realize that dream. Starting a venture requires capital and know-how. The marketplace is very competitive, and over 90 percent of new businesses starting from scratch fail within the first couple of years. It is incredibly difficult to launch a successful venture.

If you decide to start a business, you always have the option of opening a franchise. These tend to be more expensive than starting from scratch, because of the royalty and franchise fees. Any well-established franchise is going to charge you $50,000 to $100,000 just for the privilege of using their brand and systems. The most recognized franchises, like McDonald's or Burger King, cost close to a million dollars to get started once everything is said and done. Quiznos, for example, is one of the fastest-growing franchises available. You will pay $375,000 to own a sandwich shop, and in return they will guarantee—*after five years*—roughly $70,000 a year profit. You will work five to six years to recoup your investment before you can begin putting money in the bank.

Although you are not starting an eBay franchise but building your own business, the franchise model presents an interesting analogy. When people buy a franchise, they are purchasing a business system. In this book, I will outline a replicable business system you can use with a variety of products.

Quick Tip

A building is only as strong as the foundation upon which it was built—avoid building it on sand, or it will eventually crumble.

Even though you are starting small, you are still implementing systems you can use as your business grows at every level. Your listing strategies, your pricing, your customer service are all replicable for any product at any stage of the game.

It may take hundreds of thousands of dollars to open a store at your local minimall, but on eBay you can eliminate a bunch of those zeros. You can get started for as little as a few thousand dollars, and much less if you already own a computer and a digital camera. There's almost no risk. If your eBay business doesn't take off the way you expect it to initially, you're covered.

Owning and operating your own business, even as a hobby, is an amazing experience. You have no boss looking over your shoulder, no strict schedule to adhere to, and no policy manual to follow rule-by-rule. You get to do your own thing. You get to use your creativity and hard work to build your own company rather than to make someone else rich.

The benefits of owning your own business are very real, but the risks and challenges can be daunting. That's why so many people try direct sales schemes, where you sell to your family and friends and then try to get them to do the same. We've all been contacted by some of these people at one time or another.

With an eBay business, you may choose to inform people you know about it, but you won't need to for the sake of your bottom line.

Fun Fact

> You already have millions of potential customers visiting and shopping on eBay every single day.

eBay registers millions of new members every single month. You should know in advance that it's realistic to assume that whatever you plan on selling is probably already being sold on eBay. From Beanie Babies to BMWs, from old socks to new cameras, competition is abundant. Competition is good. You compete in every aspect of your life. It makes you better at whatever you choose to do. On eBay, you can learn a lot from your competition. You learn what sells and what doesn't. You learn selling, listing, pricing, and shipping strategies from your competition. Aside from your own experience, they are your absolute best tool for learning what does and doesn't work on eBay.

I received a call once from a potential competitor. He wanted to start selling pool tables on eBay and studied my business as a model. He was able to tell me exactly what I sold the previous month. He knew how many of each item I had sold, what my gross was, and his approximate estimate of my profit. His guess was frighteningly accurate. He knew the pulse of my business almost as well as I did.

Competition forces you to be more productive. Competition forces you to be more, well, competitive. Prior to writing this book, I changed my entire pool-table selling strategy on eBay. Initially, I was focused on a low-priced product imported from overseas. After two years, the competition increased, and the profit margin decreased. I altered direction to stay ahead of the curve and remain a market leader; my strategy has changed. Rather than importing product from overseas and selling product with a low-end price, I opened a new eBay store, with American-made, high-end pool tables. The reaction from the community and marketplace has been tremendous. (That User ID is LasVegas Tables.) It's an important lesson: in any selling environment, it is critical to analyze the market and stay ahead of the competition. The adage "If you continue to do what you've always done, you'll continue to get what you've always gotten" is absolutely true. Change is a fundamental basic of business success.

With competition, you set goals. I see that person and I want to sell more than they. eBay itself offers you levels of competition to strive for. PowerSellers are eBay members who sell upwards of $1,000 a month in product.

There are various levels to strive for and various benefits provided at each level. Titanium is the highest level and an excellent goal to set once your business begins to take off. No matter what level you begin at, it is important to have goals and a road map for achieving them. Write them down and begin developing a realistic step-by-step plan that will get you where you want to go. This book will help you on your way.

What do you want out of life? What are your dreams? How can eBay help you achieve those dreams? How motivated are you to make them happen?

It may sound obvious, but you must accept responsibility for the outcome of the things over which you have control. If you're driving down a road at one hundred miles per hour and you come to a fork, you have to make an instantaneous decision with no time to deliberate. Do you go left or do you go right? If your desire is to excel and succeed, you must be prepared to make decisions that affect your outcome. Otherwise, you'll keep going straight and crash and burn.

Many people are reluctant to venture into uncharted waters. They don't like to step too far outside their comfort zones.

Quick Tip

To attain success on eBay, the first step you take will be to make the decision to start.

Some people feel they're not smart enough, don't have enough money, or perhaps lack the knowledge or resources to make the leap from thinking about selling on eBay to actually doing it. The truth is, I have no idea what your eBay outcome will be. I can't guarantee success. So some people would rather pass. They inherently shy away from risk. Risk is frightening and stressful.

This, however, is where eBay is so unique. You can take the eBay risk for virtually nothing. You can experiment with the various strategies outlined in this book, with minimal investment. You can take a ride on the adventurous side with the cheapest ticket in our modern economy. There is no harm in trying even if you fail. Failure on eBay only means you should try again, this time employing a different tack. As they say, the only true failure is the failure to try.

One of the key components to success on eBay is innovation. Innovation and creativity will set you apart from the crowd. Your selling and listing strategies can distinguish you from other sellers selling the exact same items you have to offer. If you don't like the results you're getting, invent a better, smarter, simpler way of doing it. Try to think outside the box. In this book, I will provide you an in-depth, step-by-step program on how to stand out. When you identify an opportunity for innovation, muster the courage to take action. Courage is the basis for confidence. Courage is shown by launching into new adventures repeatedly and recognizing periodically that you won't always succeed. Then, when you do fail, you pick yourself right up and throw yourself back into the game. There is no failure. There is only temporary setback.

You will make mistakes. Mistakes are inevitable. The key is to learn from them and move on. If you are proud, motivated, and ready to take on the world's largest virtual marketplace, it is time to get started.

Quick Tip

Very few people out there are innovative and possess the courage to try new things and venture into the unknown. Just doing that will yield you great benefits and rewards.

Likewise, few of the people you compete with on eBay have these traits. You will see the same types of auctions over and over again. You will see the same basic incorrectly written titles, the same pictures, the same boring descriptions, the same prices and offers.

Quick Tip

For the most part, eBay is made up of casual buyers and sellers. For those select few who are serious about building a business, eBay provides the perfect foundation on which to do so.

About twelve months into my eBay selling experience, it finally became clear to me that I could do something really special on this Web site my mother drove me crazy over. It took me about eleven and a half months too long to figure out that eBay is a juggernaut with massive potential. I may be slow, but once I came around I got real serious real fast. I would like to save you from my learning curve. If I do nothing else in this book, I want to convince you of the amazing opportunity eBay presents. Turn on the mental switch in your head that says "There is great potential here and I am serious about building my business." If you remember only one thing, remember that eBay is the ultimate opportunity, and the first step is the commitment to take action—to allow yourself to open up to the possibilities of unlimited potential. Once the realization of what eBay has to offer hit me, I was in. I was hooked. I knew I had to take the plunge.

Quick Tip

It does NOT have to take YOU the twelve months it took me to figure out the opportunity provided to us by eBay.

Not long ago, a person had to drag their body out of bed, kiss their family good-bye, go off to the business world, and engage in mortal combat for ten, twelve, even fourteen hours a day. Building a business required complete and utter dedication. Success still takes hard work, but you don't have to marry your business if you follow this program. eBay has made owning a business and living a life at the same time a distinct possibility.

You don't have to be an entrepreneur to sell on eBay.

You can operate on the Web site for years without ever progressing past the hobby stage. My mother has been selling on eBay since 1998, and eBay is the most exciting hobby she's ever had. She sells to people all over the world. She has an international hobby. She buys Beanie Babies on eBay, she sells Beanie Babies on eBay, and she makes friends as she builds up her collection. My mother has a serious hobby that brings her pleasure, and eBay provides her with 115 million possible playmates.

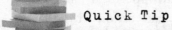

Quick Tip

> If you want eBay to help you gain financial freedom, however, you have to graduate from hobby to business.

If you want to build an asset, if you want to be eligible for valuable tax deductions, you have to set up a legitimate business. After you make the switch in your head, there are certain steps you have to take to make your plans a reality.

I recently spoke with someone who has become successful selling on eBay following the systems outlined in this book. John had never used eBay prior to learning this material. John told me that his first major revelation was the understanding that to "take eBay seriously, you have to treat it as a business right from the beginning." John is living proof that this system works. His User ID is houseofreturns.

Although an eBay business has remarkably low startup costs, there are some investments you may want to consider making in order to help your business grow. You may have some or all of the items, so your investment will be even smaller. Obviously you need a computer. If you haven't done so in a while, you may want to consider an upgrade. You don't need to have the fastest computer on the market, but it is a good idea to buy a new one about every three years. Technology is advancing all the time and the improvements can be incredibly helpful. Whether you choose a Mac or PC is up to you. On the Internet, it doesn't make a significant difference.

Another important purchase is a digital camera. When buyers shop on eBay, they can't touch, feel, inspect, or pick up the merchandise. Aside from the description you write, the photograph they see is the only evidence they get of what they're buying. Some sellers on eBay don't post photographs. This is a huge mistake. Only a small fraction of eBayers will ever bid on an item they can't see. You must use photographs in your listing, and a digital camera is the best way to take them.

In addition to a digital camera, you may find it helpful to have a scanner. You may want to use an existing photograph or a magazine article in your listing. Your item may have accompanying paperwork you wish to include. Although you can photograph these images, I have found that a scanner does come in handy occasionally.

If it is available in your area, it is a good idea to investigate signing up for a high-speed Internet connection. You will be on the Internet all the time. You'll post listings, check your auctions, research your competition, ad infinitum. A high-speed connection will make a huge difference in your life and costs only a few dollars more than dial-up. It is also great to have a cordless phone. If you're talking to customers or vendors or anyone else and you're cordless, you can walk around multitasking instead of sitting there waiting for the calls to be over before you can complete other items on your to-do list. You can make yourself a cup of coffee while placing an order or placating a customer, all in your bathrobe and slippers.

One purchase people don't think about, which can make a considerable difference, is a comfortable chair. You'll be spending a lot of time sitting in front of your computer, and a comfortable chair can save you muscle pain and chiropractor bills. Ergonomic comfort in your workstation is a definite plus. When I started out on eBay, I bought a really nice keyboard and mouse. The more time you spend on the Internet and at your computer, the more these things become part of who you are and what you do. My mouse is like an extension of my hand. My wife tells me they're going to have to get it surgically removed one of these days.

When you set up your home office, give it a professional look. When you walk into the space you've dedicated to your eBay venture first thing in the morning, if it looks like an office and feels like an office, you're going to be more productive. Psychologically, a business environment surrounding you will help create a professional spirit inside of you.

You should also think about how you're going to ship your items. You might want to stock up on some basic packing materials, such as boxes, tape, Styrofoam peanuts and bubble wrap, not to mention a tape measure and postal scale to measure and weigh your packages from home.

Compared to leasing property, hiring employees, advertising, and ordering considerable inventory, these costs are insignificant.

These items are all business expenses and therefore deductible. If you want to save some money, you can buy them on eBay and learn even more about the Web site from the buyer's perspective. I also advocate buying whatever you can on eBay. Support the community that is supporting you. Plus, buying on eBay is the easiest way to build up that crucial feedback score when you're first starting out, a subject I'll delve into in great depth in chapter 8.

As you are making your first business purchases, it is also a good idea to start thinking about how you're going to manage your business from your home. For tax pur-

Things You Need to Start "Working" on eBay

1. Relatively up-to-date computer
2. Digital camera
3. Scanner
4. High-speed Internet connection
5. Cordless phone
6. Comfortable chair
7. Nice keyboard and mouse
8. Some shipping supplies (i.e., boxes, packing tape, bubble wrap, tape measure, and postal scale)

poses, you need to dedicate a portion of your home exclusively to your business if you want it to qualify for a tax deduction. After choosing a workspace, think about how you want to organize it. You will need a simple filing system and basic office supplies.

If you plan on storing your own inventory, you will need a storage area and a place to do all of your packaging. Consider creating a minimailroom where you can store your packing materials and stage your shipping operations.

One important element in treating your eBay activities as a legitimate business is proper recordkeeping. Keep a file for receipts. Keep track of important outgoing and incoming paperwork. I will discuss this in detail in later chapters, but recordkeeping is important both for tax purposes and for your ability to track and analyze your growing business.

It is also important to set goals and devise a game plan. Perhaps in the very beginning you plan on selling only one or two items a week. Set a date by which you plan to be selling one item a day. Then decide when you want to increase that to two or three items a day. Build gradually over time, but set a schedule. It is a process that could take up to six months or more.

If you were to decide to start a traditional bricks-and-mortar business, it could take you six months to a year just to arrive at your grand opening. You'd have to write up business plans and projections, raise capital, secure a lease on a space, order inventory, and so on. It is a time-consuming process.

On eBay, you can experiment and profit from day one, yielding the tax benefits from a home-based business while still learning the ins and outs of the marketplace and your enterprise.

The tax benefits of an eBay business alone can add three, four, or five thousand dollars to your bottom line this year, if you just implement the strategies outlined in this book. Everyone can benefit from them, regardless of whether their business is profitable or not.

If you aren't sure whether you really want to get serious about your eBay business, you can start by selling part-time. You can keep your current job and experiment with eBay a few hours in the evenings or on weekends. You can experiment with different strategies and different products, seeing what works and what doesn't, through trial and error. One of the benefits of eBay is that you can list a few things, play around, and if something sells well, you have the choice to continue carrying that product. You don't have to risk much at all to make a go at it. Even part-time, you will still reap the tax benefits available to home-based businesses. You can earn a small profit and save on taxes while earning your current salary.

Considering tax benefits, starting an eBay business makes all the sense in the world. There's no reason *not* to do it. An employee earning $25,000 a year decides to start a part-time eBay business. That employee is now eligible for a number of deductions that will directly lead to more money in his pocket or bank account. You can save that money, spend it, or reinvest it in your eBay business. Instead of paying the government that extra money, you can decide whom you want to give it to, be it your bank account, your product vendors, or DisneyWorld. This is a legitimate way to save on the single highest expense every one of us has—taxes.

Most of us have been taught that if you want to make more money, you have to work harder. Now, you can work only a few extra hours a week by establishing a home-based business and save an incredible amount of money, as long as you do it the right way.

Quick Tip

> This is not a way to avoid paying the taxes you rightfully owe. This is a way to legitimately reduce your taxable income.

In chapter 10, I outline all the steps you have to take to establish your business and qualify for valuable deductions. When I was starting out, I had no idea about any of these things, and I wish I had. I could have saved a great deal right from the beginning if I had had this information from the get-go. The steps and strategies in this book will help you create your business, fine-tune it, and accelerate to the next level. If you haven't made your first sale yet, what you'll learn here will get you on your way. If you're already selling on eBay, let your enthusiasm and the strategies herein allow you to climb as high as you need to reach your loftiest goals.

eBay is a golden opportunity

- Low start-up costs
- Low overhead
- Minimal risk
- Huge global marketplace—115 million customers and counting!
- Do it part-time or full-time or anywhere in between
- Lucrative tax benefits
- Think like an entrepreneur
- Set up an office at home
- Buy your eBay tools on eBay
- Set up a filing system and keep good records
- Start tonight!

Part Two

First
Steps

CHAPTER THREE

What to Sell

Over the last few years, I have talked to thousands of people about eBay. Almost to a person, the first question they ask is, "What do I sell?" Even more than how to get started on eBay or what steps they need to take to set up their business, people want to know what product to sell and where to find it. For first-timers, I have one universal suggestion. Think about everything you have in your house, every single possession you own. The first item you should sell on eBay is the one thing you are absolutely, 100 percent positive no one will ever buy.

Think of the craziest thing that you have, something you would gladly give away if someone would just come pick it up. It's something you hide from company and are too embarrassed to give away to charity. If someone buys *that* thing from you, I guarantee you will be hooked. That's it. It's over for you. If some eBayer pays you actual money for this monkey on your back, you will be an instant convert. For me it was a thousand-pound pool table. For you it might be your husband's naked-lady mud flap barstools or the Tiki grass-skirt lamp your sister brought you back from Hawaii. Whatever it is, it's an eBay moment of truth. There will be more.

After you've bid fond farewell to your Krups coffee grinder with a busted top and no grinding ability whatsoever and shipped it off to a curiously satisfied customer, you have to figure out what to sell next. There is a fundamental step that everyone takes at this juncture. Everything in your house you can stand parting with gets listed on eBay. You clean the joint out. For many people, that could take weeks or even months. This is not necessarily a part-time gig. Everyone has a house full of what some people call "old junk." I call it "treasures"—your preowned, vintage, experienced product that you are using to start your new eBay business. You can now refer

---

eBay Fun Facts

1. "On eBay in 2003, more than 20 Von Dutch hats sold for $900 plus"—*Los Angeles Times,* January 2003
2. "Virtually an online trunk show—the first of its kind"— *New York Times,* January 2003
3. eBay is ranked the #1 fashion site on the Internet
4. Health & Beauty grew 88 percent in 2003 from 2002

to these treasures as bona fide inventory. We're going to clear this inventory on eBay.

Some people have great difficulty getting rid of things. Believe it or not, the American Psychiatric Association has recognized "hoarding" as one manifestation of obsessive-compulsive disorder.

Quick Tip

Not that you need to start taking Paxil if you're a particularly excessive hoarder, but selling things on eBay might be a practical step for you, and it's cheaper than therapy.

I say this in half-jest. My friend Danny actually was diagnosed with exactly this type of OCD, and part of his cognitive-behavioral therapy program included selling his once-precious but useless belongings on eBay. Cursed with the packrat gene, my grandparents filled their basement with forty years of life's treasures. When they didn't use it anymore, they put it in the basement. They didn't give it away, they didn't throw it away, they didn't sell it. I could make a fortune on eBay selling what used to take up a corner of that room.

Your perception of the world around you is about to change. I know, because this happened to me. It's profound. You'll start to look at things in your home differently. Once the reality shift sets in, you will look around as you rummage through your house and say to yourself, "Hey, I can sell that on eBay!"

This is just phase one of your new reality. Eventually,

and perhaps unfortunately, you will sell just about every-thing in your home. The real kicker, however, is what happens when you go to your friends, neighbors, and rel-atives' houses. You can be assured that you'll be thinking about the items you see on their bookshelves, counters, and so on, and ask yourself—and maybe ask them—"Can I sell this for you on eBay?"

Little dollar signs start spinning through your eyes like the wheels of a slot machine, and you begin calculat-ing what you could sell their vintage spool collection for.

Quick Tip

Allow yourself to open up to the possibility that saleable product is all around.

---

eBay can be your own personal Antique Road Show. Perhaps that box of old coins your great-uncle Oscar left you are actually worth something. A gentleman came to one of my seminars. He had sleeves and sleeves of McDonald's paper cups from the sixties. It turns out people collect them, and he sells them one at a time for $12 to $15 apiece.

Make eBay Work for You

As you're going through your belongings looking for things to sell, you'll find it helpful to use eBay as a research tool. You can run a completed-item search and see how items exactly like or similar to yours have been selling recently. This will give you some idea as to the value of your item as a commodity on eBay. In addition, I have developed the zTemplates Market Research Wizard that I will discuss in chapter 11. Included in these research tools is a "Price Finder," which provides the price your item will probably fetch before you list it. The "Price Finder" is more accurate than a completed-item search and more comprehensive, as it provides more data per item across a larger span of time—specifically, from the latest data available back to the beginning of eBay. Also, using these tools is less time-consuming than running completed-item searches, because all the data you are looking for is analyzed and condensed on a single page. zTemplates Market Research Wizard uses closed eBay auction data to provide users with unparalleled information and intelligence on the eBay marketplace. Successful sellers can now focus more on selling and less on manual searches that may or may not provide accurate information.

Knowing the projected price of your item is extremely useful, no matter what you are selling or where and how you acquired it. You can determine what your opening bid should be, what kind of profit margin to expect, and whether listing it will be worth the time, effort, and costs required. This will tell you whether or not you should invest in the item in the first place.

Before you go to throw something out, consider selling it on eBay.

If you have clothes that don't fit anymore or are out of style, consider selling them. I just sold my very used four-year-old sneakers for $21. If you got married any time in the last ten years, there has to be a pile of unwanted gifts sitting around somewhere. If your kids have outgrown their clothes or ignore the toys they're too old for, list them. Anything you don't use or doesn't work anymore is now eBay fodder.

Many people get started on eBay as a hobby before it becomes their business. They sign on, sell a few items, and then use the money that goes into their PayPal account to buy other things. My wife is the perfect example of this. She uses eBay to support her shopping habit. She sells so she can buy. The more she sells, the more she can buy. I ask her how her business is doing and she always says, "Great." She loves eBay. I pay for all of her clothes. When she no longer wants them, she sells them on eBay and keeps the money. She collects shipping and handling, but always has me take the items to my office to ship. She has no overhead, no expenses, and 110 percent profits. It's the best eBay business ever.

She uses it, however, simply to rotate her wardrobe.
She buys clothes, wears them for a few months,
sells them, and then uses the money to start the
whole process over again.

She recently bought a pair of Ugg slippers for $33. They didn't fit, and she ended up reselling them for $110. She understands how to use eBay and make it work for her. She sold a lot of six used lipsticks for $72. My belongings are game for her, too. Recently she came to me and said, "You know that cologne that I bought you? Don't use it anymore. I'm selling it on eBay. I'm putting together a set of colognes."

"It's half used. It has no cap," I said. Needless to say, I have no more cologne because she sold them all. I thought maybe she would buy me a new bottle—no such luck.

Women want to rotate their wardrobe every six months. Men want to do the same thing with electronics. We can sell our old cell phones and get new ones that take pictures. We can sell our VCRs and get DVD players or TiVo. Replace our old computer with the new one that walks, talks, and juggles in its spare time. In essence, selling old stuff creates a fund for buying new, which can then be resold again when it becomes old. The cycle is endless. The market demand on eBay is for both brand-new items as well as preowned treasures. All is fair game on eBay.

Fun Facts

1. 2 video game consoles sell every minute
2. 14 DVDs sell every minute
3. 2,500 children's VHS tapes sell every day
4. 2,900 rare books sell every day

While you are out looking for product to sell, it is helpful to keep in mind what is already successful on eBay. There are six categories that sell over a billion dollars a year on the Web site. In no specific order, they include:

- Electronics
- Sporting goods
- Housewares
- Jewelry
- Collectibles

The #1 category on eBay is eBay Motors

It may be hard to believe that the number one category on eBay would be cars. A few years ago, the staff at eBay was having a roundtable meeting, and one employee suggested creating an automotive category. The response he got was immediate laughter. They couldn't believe that people would buy something on eBay that huge, that needs to be test-driven, checked by a mechanic, and possibly shipped out of state. I didn't think I could sell pool tables. They didn't think they could sell cars. We were both wrong.

Words of Wisdom

"One can get anything if he is willing to help enough others get what they want."
—*Zig Ziglar, salesman*

eBay Motors is the largest online seller of cars in the world. In 2002 and 2003, I held the same distinction with pool tables. It turns out that people love buying and selling cars on eBay. Buyers don't have to deal with used-car salesmen, and sellers know they're getting a fair price for their vehicle, reaching a much wider audience than they would advertising in the newspaper. Often cars are sold to buyers in the same region, who do come and test-drive, but just as often they're sold out of state.

Another very large category, which is not a billion-dollar category yet but is growing at a very rapid pace, is eBay Real Estate. People are buying and selling investment properties, commercial properties, time shares, residential properties, and so on. Unless it's not allowed, anything can be sold on eBay. If you have an item you're skeptical about because of its size or feasibility, give it a try. It will probably sell.

This new perception I have warned you about—it's real and it's a byproduct of reading this book. You will forever think about things differently.

It's not only in your home and your friends' and relatives' homes. You walk through shopping malls and pass garage sales on Sunday morning on the way to brunch. Wherever you go, whatever you see, you will think, "I can sell that on eBay." Your whole perspective of the world will change. It's a wonderful thing.

Look at the World Through eBay-colored Glasses

Once your house looks like two repo men have spent a very successful afternoon carting off everything you own, it's time to start thinking about what you're going to sell from now on. Use your new eBay perspective to your advantage. Next time you leave the house, think about the situations, people, and objects you encounter. Frame them with respect to a potential eBay business. The reality is that anything and everything is sold on eBay. When you go into Macy's next time to buy shoes, and you see a 75 percent off closeout sale, think to yourself, "I can buy this for seventy-five percent off retail, go sell it for half off on eBay, and make twenty-five percent." Look around and you will find product surrounding you everywhere.

The opportunity is unlimited if you have that mental framework. Open your mind and look at the clues around you, at home, on your way to work, at the mall, on vacation, ad infinitum. When you are out Sunday and you do happen to see that sign on the lamppost that says "garage sale," don't just keep going. It's OK to be a little late to brunch. Stop by. You'll be amazed at the treasures. People often have absolutely no idea what they have lurking in their closets. They just want it out. You'll find collectibles priced at a fraction of what they're worth, and then sell them on eBay, where people know too well and will pay whatever it takes. If a store has a going-out-of-business sale, get out of your car, take a look and see what's there. Finding product to make your eBay hobby your eBay business is actually a very simple transition. The first step is opening your eyes and ears to the possibilities out there.

In San Diego, I met a young man who goes to garage sales every weekend, looking for videotapes and DVDs.

He buys any videotape and DVD priced at fifty cents or less. If it's more than fifty cents, he walks away. The reason he does this is that he has a contact who will buy any video he has for a dollar. He's happy, because he makes such a large profit margin. The contact he sells to, however, sells them on eBay for ten to fifteen dollars apiece. I asked the young man why he didn't just sell them on eBay himself and he wasn't interested. You may find someone like this, who is willing to go out and do all the searching for you so you can make the larger profit.

There are so many great garage-sale stories, I couldn't begin to tell them all here. The diamonds in the rough are out there every weekend just waiting to be found. I worked with another young man, who found a Tiffany clock at a garage sale. He had no idea what it was but knew the word Tiffany because he had a younger sister. He was already buying some books and asked the seller how much he wanted for the clock. He threw it in for an extra five dollars. He listed it at $0.01 with no reserve, assuming it would sell for more than his five-dollar investment. He really had no idea what he had. Six hours after listing it, he got an offer via e-mail from a man who wanted to buy it for two hundred dollars. After thinking about it, he realized the clock may be worth something.

He finally did the research he should have done right from the beginning and found three identical clocks selling for two to three thousand dollars each.

Since he hadn't received any bids, he edited his listing to provide a link to those auctions to show people what his clock was worth. The offers started pouring in. A Good Samaritan sent an e-mail telling him all about his clock and explaining why his wasn't worth quite as much as the other three. His five-dollar garage-sale clock ended up selling for $1,550.

Recently, at a seminar, a young woman told the audience about her garage-sale experience. Most of what she sells on eBay she finds at garage sales. One particular Sunday, she bought two bronze statues with gold-leaf foil surrounding the top. She purchased both for $20. She sold both on eBay. The first sold for $1,300 and the other for $2,000, and those numbers are not typos. It's undeniable—eBay is FUN!

I'll tell you one more garage-sale story, just because I love these. A friend of mine passed by a garage sale on a Sunday morning a few months ago. He didn't see anything interesting and was about to walk away when he saw a box labeled "Transformers" under a pile of other things. He pulled it out and rummaged through it. There were seven or eight Transformers in the lot, most with broken pieces. He tried to control his excitement when, at the bottom of the box, he saw a square resembling a tape player. Could this be the holy grail of Transformers collectors—Soundwave? He carefully picked it up and confirmed that it was. Miraculously, it was one of two in the box in almost perfect condition. As calmly as possible, he asked the bored man barely awake in his beach chair how much he was asking for the lot. The man looked at him like he was crazy. He couldn't imagine what a grown man would want with a box of broken toys. All he wanted was $2.50 for all of it. My friend handed him three dollars, waited patiently for his two quarters in change, and promptly sold Soundwave on eBay for $810. He already had one anyway. People have no idea what they have. Use their ignorance to make a fortune on eBay.

Recently I was on a cruise in the Mediterranean. As it happens, I got into a conversation about eBay, and, of course, one of the first questions asked was "What would I sell?" I had an idea. I said, "Let's do an experiment. I always say product is everywhere. We're in Mykonos, Greece. Let's try it." We walked into a local jewelry store where the salespeople spoke excellent English. We sat down with them, bought a necklace, and said, "Have you guys ever thought about selling on the Internet, on eBay, taking this jewelry you make by hand and selling it worldwide instead of to your small market here on this tiny island?" Within thirty minutes, I had contact infor-

eBay Fun Fact—Stamps

1. An 1851 Canadian 12 pence stamp sold for $34,000
2. The most common search keyword in 2003 was Hong Kong
3. The largest category is United States
4. The fastest-growing category is Africa
5. A stamp item is sold every 15 seconds
6. Over 400,000 new listings per month

mation, a wholesale price list, and a new product to sell. The experiment, as I predicted, was an easy success.

What Do You Know?

When you ask, the question of what to sell on eBay, the answer may lie inside you—in your background, your interests, your strengths, and your weaknesses.

If there's anything left in your house after you sold everything on eBay, use it as research material. We often think of the things around our house as being mundane or perhaps overly familiar. We choose these things, however, as a reflection of who we are. The things we put in our home are usually the things we're passionate about. Think about what it is that you're fascinated by, that you're interested in, and that's going to point to the things that you have an understanding of and talent for. If you collect belt buckles, for example, you may really have a feel for the market and know what belt buckles will and won't sell and what people will pay for them. If you understand a market already, that may be an excellent place to start.

Try Different Things

Although it may help to sell what you are interested in, this is absolutely not a requirement. You don't even have to like your product as long as other people seem to. eBay is an incredible tool. If you decide to open a store in the minimall selling beauty supplies, you have to invest a significant amount of money before you can sell one hairbrush. You'll have to sign a lease, set up the store, purchase inventory, hire staff, prepare an advertising campaign, and so on. The average start-up cost for an average business in the United States is $250,000. A franchise, as I mentioned before, may cost you double that, and none of this investment guarantees you will ever even make your money back. Three months into your beauty-supply business, you may realize that the market is not nearly what you thought it was going to be, and you will not be able to turn a profit. Switching to another product—computers or children's clothing or anything else you may think of—will cost almost as much as your original investment cost you.

On eBay, this is not the case at all. You have the freedom to experiment. Try hairbrushes this week. Sell three or five or ten of them. Check out how other people are doing, with a completed-item search or by using the zTemplates Market Research Wizard. If they don't sell, get out of the hairbrush business this week and into the cell phone business next week. The week after that you can try children's clothing. You have no overhead. Your only investment is your listing fees and the few items of inventory you need to conduct your experiment. If an item doesn't sell, it's not a big deal. Move on to the next. If it sells, you're in business, and soon you may find you're the largest hairbrush vendor on eBay. It is an amazing opportunity, to be able to find out what works and what doesn't, with minimal risk and investment.

Product, the eBay Way

In any selling environment, there are two basic philosophies, or approaches, to choose from. The first involves low volume and high profit-margin. An example of this is a very high-end furniture store. If they sell one $10,000 couch in a day, they're happy. The second is the opposite—high volume, low profit-margin. This is the Costco/Target approach and also what most eBayers subscribe to. Buyers on eBay are looking for a deal. They've done their research and they want a better price than they can get in a bricks-and-mortar store. Because of this, sellers on eBay have to have better prices than what's out there unless an item is in such high demand that people are just grateful to have the opportunity to purchase it. To create a successful business with a low profit-margin, it is necessary to sell more product than if you were able to charge retail price. Wal-Mart can afford to sell compact discs cheaper than anyone else because they sell more of them than anyone in the world. Decide what your approach will be but keep in mind that historically, on eBay, this high-volume-low-margin philosophy tends to be the more successful.

As you move from hobby to business, there are two things to consider when choosing your product. The first crucial factor in your decision is what the item sells for on eBay and how much you will have to pay for the honor of selling it. If you can purchase your product for below the average eBay selling price, you have margin and you're in business. If not, try to find something else.

The second factor is the availability or supply of the item you want to sell. Depending on the profit margin you have determined you can expect, you will need a certain amount of that product to be able to sell enough to be successful. If you want to sell this product long-term, you also want to consider how available the inventory will continue to be to you. If you can expect a decent profit margin and have access to enough of the product to get your business going, this may be the perfect product to sell.

There is a third factor you might want to consider, even though I haven't done so in my own business. I recommend finding product that is what I call "UPS-able." Pool tables are not "UPS-able." Because of the size of my items, instead of being able to use one of the traditional shipping methods, I have to use a freight company to ship to my customers. One of the cornerstones of good customer service on eBay is fast shipping. I cannot control this, because I rely on a freight company. Of all the negative feedback I get, 99.9 percent is related to problems with the speed of shipping. When we started selling watches, I was relieved to be able to control my shipping by using UPS. The amount of negative feedback received in our watch store is a fraction of that received in our billiards store. So I recommend a product that will yield a profit margin, is available in large enough quantity, and is "UPS-able." Still, there is the question of where to find that product, and I will delve into that further now.

Trading Assistant

After selling your own things, one natural transition is to start selling other people's things. Just as you have a house filled with treasure to be sold, so do your family, friends, and neighbors. This alone can create a sea of unlimited inventory. eBay has a valuable and innovative feature called the Trading Assistant Program. Trading assistants are people who officially sell other people's treasures on eBay. A great number of eBayers were selling on consignment long before eBay ever got involved officially. The powers-that-be recognized the phenomenon, however, and wanted to create a program to help these people succeed on an even greater level.

There are a few criteria one must meet to become an official eBay trading assistant. First, you must have a feedback rating of fifty or more, so to build this up you need to sell or buy as quickly as possible. Next, that feedback rating has to consist of 97 percent positive comments. If someone is not a competent and reliable transactioneer, eBay doesn't want them in this program. If you provide good customer service, ship quickly, describe your items accurately, and pay quickly as a buyer, you will find that 97 percent is rather simple to achieve. In addition, you have to have sold four items in the past thirty days. Finally, trading assistants must uphold the eBay values and be upstanding members of the community. You can accomplish this by following the rules and avoiding too many complaints.

To sell other people's treasures on consignment, you don't have to be an official eBay trading assistant, but there

*are benefits to getting qualified and joining the program.
The first step to take when you meet the minimum
requirements for this program is to set up a trading assistant account by clicking the "Become an Assistant" link
from the Trading Assistants Directory.*

Once you have created your account, eBay will
include you in the Trading Assistants Directory I just
mentioned. This is just like running a classified ad for
your services. People who want the aid of a trading assistant in selling their objects will search the directory for
assistants in their area. This is your chance to tell the
world you are available to sell anything they don't want
anymore.

Trading assistants are not employees or independent
contractors of eBay and at no point will eBay endorse or
approve a trading assistant. As I have mentioned before,
eBay provides a level playing field with no specific buyer
or seller receiving special services or privileges. This is
true of the trading assistant program as well. Where a

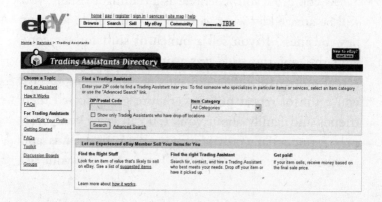

trading assistant appears in the directory is based on experience and transaction volume. The higher your feedback score, the higher on the list you'll appear. The program is essentially an advertising tool. As a trading assistant, you run your own independent business free from any involvement from eBay.

Selling as a trading assistant allows you to leverage your selling expertise without having to find product yourself. Clients provide all your inventory and you are compensated for your efforts on terms you both agree to. There is no limit to the number of clients you can have or the size of the inventory available to you. There are a number of brick-and-mortar companies popping up around the country that you may worry about as competition. They will take your items and sell them for you if you bring them into the store. If we are assuming that someone is inherently lazy enough or lacks the skills to sell their items themselves, I have trouble believing they will even want to load them up in their car and drive them to some store. If you, as a trading assistant, pick up items from your clients, you are already ten steps ahead of these companies.

As you grow your clientele as a trading assistant, you will be amazed by what word of mouth will do for your new business. If you sell a bunch of stuff for someone who thought the stuff was worthless and return with actual money for them, not only are they going to give you a ton of repeat business, they're going to tell their friends and family about you. You can grow your business exponentially just starting with your friends and family. You'll start to get calls. "I'm a cousin of your sister's hairstylist. I know you don't know me, but I heard you sell stuff for people on eBay. I could really use your help. I have a spare room filled with crap and I really want to turn the room into an office." This will happen all the time. You may even have to turn away clients or start hiring help to handle all the inventory coming your way.

If you are having trouble finding clients, however, you may want to consider running a classified ad in your local newspaper. You could write something like "I WILL SELL YOUR ITEMS," or "ITEMS FOR SALE? I WILL SELL THEM FOR YOU." You can solicit phone calls from customers and offer to sell their unwanted things. We've discussed how everyone has inventory just sitting around their house. Many people are too busy or disinclined to sell their own things. Perhaps they don't know what their items are worth and are concerned about getting a fair price. There are millions of people who don't use a computer. You can sell their belongings for them.

The Trading Assistant Program provides complete flexibility. When you sign up as a trading assistant, you are essentially advertising your own independent listing service to potential clients. Since it's an independent service between you and your client, the two of you are in charge of negotiating all the terms. It is important, however, that you negotiate all the details in advance, before you begin working with your client. Make sure you both agree what the start price of the auctions will be, who pays eBay fees, who ships the item, what happens if an item doesn't sell, etc.

Trading assistant fees can vary by item type, size, and

price. You may decide to charge a percentage, like a traditional consignment store. Perhaps you will want to set some sort of minimum fees or charge ancillary fees for additional services you offer. For example, you might say, "I charge $50 to pick up items at your home in my truck and then a flat fee for every item I sell with you paying all listing fees regardless of whether an item sells or not." The key thing is that fees are in your control and that you negotiate upfront how you are going to handle those fees with each client. Another point to remember is that, regardless of how you handle fees with the client, you are ultimately responsible for all eBay fees, since you are the formal seller from eBay's perspective and these fees will appear on your eBay billing statement. As a trading assistant, you still want to follow all of the rules and strategies outlined elsewhere in this book. You will be the seller. Your User ID will appear, and your feedback will be affected. It is a good idea to conduct your consignment business exactly as you would if you paid for the inventory in advance.

Wholesale Lots

Quick Tip

People are always surprised when I say this, but the best place to find things to sell on eBay is on eBay itself.

My mother buys 90 percent of the Beanie Babies she sells on eBay. One of the phenomenal things about this

Web site that once shared space with Ebola virus information is that it is becoming a stock market for objects. My mother definitely understands the concept of buy low and sell high. The true value of an item is what someone will pay for it. These values are set for almost everything, every single day on eBay. Supply and demand are by far the two most important words in the world of eBay.

The best place on eBay to buy product for resale is a section called "Wholesale Lots."

The "Wholesale" link on eBay's home page will take you directly there.

You can actually buy groups of items at wholesale prices and then resell them one by one at closer to retail price. I sell scooters on eBay. I don't sell them one at a time, though. I sell them in lots of six, twelve, eighteen, and twenty-four. Two types of people buy my scooters—retail dealers who want to experiment with new products in their stores but don't want to invest in a large inventory until they know it works; and people who want to sell scooters on eBay but don't have a retail store or access to a wholesaler through traditional channels. They buy from me and are immediately in the scooter business.

If you want to sell Sony computers, but you're not an authorized Sony dealer in a retail store in a protected territory, you can't be an authorized Sony dealer. On eBay, however, you can go to Wholesale Lots, then to electronics, computers, and finally Sony, and you'll find Sony lots for sale. Perhaps the seller used to work for Sony or has access to closeouts. They don't have the time or the inclination to

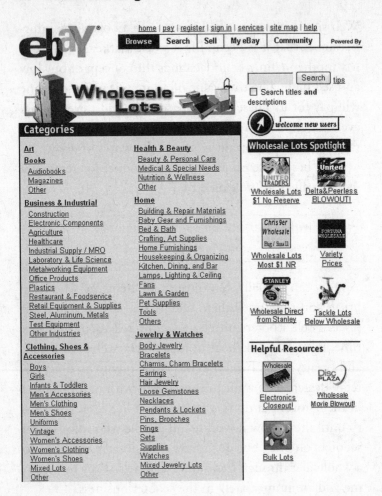

sell them one at a time. They want to sell the bunch and get out. Many people don't think of eBay as a place to buy wholesale, but it is actually an excellent resource.

There is another great benefit to buying wholesale lots on eBay. You often end up with a somewhat rare product. Many people with eBay businesses use drop-shipping companies. In this situation, you are the middleman. You list and sell the item, and the drop-shipping company ships it wherever you tell them to. You never see the inventory. But the problem with drop-shipping is that a great number of people on eBay are using the drop-shipping companies. There are only so many of them. Everyone has the same inventory. You'll see hundreds of auctions selling the exact same item.

By contrast, wholesale lots on eBay are sold by many different kinds of people for many different reasons. Perhaps a small souvenir store on Nantucket is shutting down for the season and wants to get rid of some extra inventory. Perhaps someone ordered a hundred too many candles for their big, fancy outdoor wedding. Whatever the reason, there is a great variety of things being sold in wholesale lots, and you can narrow down the competition considerably by selling something everyone else doesn't necessarily have.

To help wholesale buyers and sellers find each other, eBay has improved and expanded the wholesale lots category structure. They add new categories to the structure every month. As a result, there are now over one hundred different wholesale lots categories, located in each of the major categories in which wholesale trading is available on the site. This consistent naming and placement have made it easier for reseller buyers to find the product they are looking for. The wholesale lots categories are actually spread throughout eBay's category structure. Each major category on eBay now has its own wholesale lots subcategory.

The success of the Wholesale Lots category on eBay has been extensive, as evidenced by the dramatic growth it has undergone since its inception.

Fun Fact

In the last year, listings in the wholesale categories have grown from about eleven thousand to well over forty thousand available at any given time, and gross merchandise sales have grown by 465 percent year after year!

Product Is EVERYWHERE

Aside from your own or others' treasures and the wholesale lots available on eBay, there are a number of very simple sources of product. As I mentioned before, garage sales—and their fancy cousins, estate sales—or auctions are valuable places to start. Thrift shops, flea markets, and discount stores like Marshall's or Ross can also provide inventory at greatly reduced prices. If you live in upstate New York, come September, your local discount store may start selling bathing suits at 50 percent or more off the already discounted price. Those bathing suits may be useless in the Catskills, but in Miami Beach it's still eighty degrees and people there would love a great deal on a new bikini to wear to the beach.

Expanding on this concept, one great idea is to buy

out of season and sell in season. The day after Christmas, every ornament, every icicle light, every singing Santa Claus doll goes on sale for a fraction of what it sold for in November. Retailers are dying to get rid of the stuff, because everyone has overdosed on ham and "Jingle Bells" by this point and can barely see red and green together without feeling a little woozy. They also want to move in that Valentine's Day merchandise so you can spend a month and a half agonizing over what will satisfy your girlfriend or feeling miserable because you don't have one. If you have the room to store it for a year, buy up all that Christmas product and start selling it come next November. This strategy can work for any seasonal items you come across.

Often department stores and small businesses alike end up with merchandise they just can't seem to move. You can speak to the managers of these establishments about buying all of their closeout items in bulk. They need the room for product they can sell, and you can find customers in different markets who are just dying for these types of items. If you approach the manager of every store in the mall, you're bound to get at least one taker, possibly more. For a few hundred or thousand dollars, depending on the investment you want to make, you can acquire entire lots of items to sell. This is another great place to use that completed-item search or Market Research Wizard tool. Find out what the manager wants for his closeout items. Ask him to hold them for a couple of hours, and go back to your computer to do some homework. If these items are selling for more than the manager wants, and you can make a profit, go back and buy them. If not, see if you can renegotiate or move on to another store.

Become a Broker

An alternative to buying the manager's closeout inventory is to become his broker. Acting as a broker is similar to selling on consignment as a trading assistant, with three distinct differences. If you are a trading assistant, most of the items you sell will be used. If you are a broker, your inventory is brand-new. If you are a trading assistant, your clients are individuals comprising friends, family, friends of friends, people who found you through the Trading Assistant Program or your Web site, and so on. If you are a broker, your relationships are exclusively with businesses. The final distinction is that as a broker, you do not sell anything on consignment. The store maintains possession of the item until you sell it.

You draw up a wholesale list with the owner or manager, a price somewhere above his cost but well below retail. You then list the item on eBay and, when it sells, return to the store and purchase it at the previously stated price before heading off to UPS to ship it. The difference between the final auction price and the price you pay for the item is your profit. Much like a trading assistant, you invest no money in the inventory and never actually have to store it.

Over the past two years, some of my most successful eBay ventures have come from relationships in which I acted as an eBay broker. One of my goals as a seller is, and has been, to sell name-brand products. It's very difficult, and in some cases almost impossible, to sell name-brand items unless you are a retailer. For example, Sony, Canon, and Minolta are all name-brand electronics manufacturers who would not sell directly to me. In order for me to sell these products, I had to create an eBay broker relationship.

Earlier I mentioned that your perspective would change with regard to the world around you. I discussed how you would start seeing eBay selling opportunities around you all the time. This happened to me about two years ago. I was in a cell phone store, having a conversation with the manager. He asked me what I did, and I explained that I sold pool tables on eBay, along with a few other miscellaneous items. He had this idea that maybe I could sell some of his excess inventory for him. It was this experience that really opened my eyes to the power of this eBay broker concept. Here I was, suddenly in the cellular phone business. I had no store, no overhead, no inventory, yet I was selling name-brand cell phones, such as Nokia, Samsung, and Sony Ericsson.

This strategy may be the most powerful method to sell on eBay with unlimited inventory. There are over twenty million small businesses in the United Sates. Almost none of them sell on eBay. You have the power to enable these small-business owners to move more product and increase their profits while you sell their items on their behalf.

Sometimes you'll have tremendous success and sometimes you won't, but there is no risk in trying. There is no risk in experimenting with various products from your local neighborhood retail stores. Store owners are in the retail business, not the eBay business.

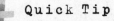

Quick Tip

> They don't *want* to deal with, or may not *know how* to deal with, the nuances of selling on eBay. This is the service you provide them. It would be more cost-effective for them to outsource the job to you.

They are grateful because they're selling more, and you get unlimited, but no physical, inventory. It's an arrangement that benefits everyone. The best part of this program is that it doesn't matter what the products are as long as you have two things: adequate margin and ample supply. This program works with the local cell phone store, electronics store, clothing store, bookstore, or candle-making store. Become an eBay broker and discover the world of unlimited eBay inventory.

In chapter 1, I discussed the self-titled hippie-gypsies who planned on running their eBay business out of their van while they roamed the world, allowing the wind to take them where it wished. Filled with curiosity, I asked them the question that everyone asks me. "What are you going to sell?" Unlike most people who come to my seminars, they already had an answer. They have a friend who goes to India all the time and buys beautiful handmade items at dirt-cheap prices. She asks for her cost plus a tiny extra, plus the shipping and handling, and everything they make after that is pure profit for them. They showed me small purses that my wife tells me are very trendy right now. They list them for $0.50, which is what the woman charges them and they keep every penny it sells for above that. In addition, the woman takes care of the shipping and handling. They have unlimited inventory they never have to touch. They may call themselves hippie-gypsies, but I call them very clever businesspeople.

Product Sourcing

A phrase with eBay sellers that's really hot right now is "product sourcing." Through product sourcing you can create relationships with vendors who will actually inventory your merchandise and then ship it for you. Through this method, you would create a relationship with a vendor, or vendors, who would supply you the information and the pictures of the items. You would list the items on eBay. Once the item is sold, you fax or e-mail the order, pay for the item (with the money paid to you by your new customer), and then your vendor ships for you.

The benefit of this program is that there is no inventory and virtually no overhead whatsoever. Once I added this to my inventory formula, I realized it was the final piece—the topper—of the unlimited inventory puzzle. These product sources are typically found in product-sourcing directories, which can be found on the Internet if you search hard enough. There are a lot of them out there. The key is to participate in a directory that's affordable *and* that has reliable product sources. The best wholesale product-sourcing directories I have used can be found at auctionproductsources.com.

The product is out there. Whether you sell new or used, your own or someone else's, the possibilities are truly endless. As soon as you put down this book, you will see potential auctions wherever you go. You'll automatically think about keywords, descriptions, and eye the item for the box size you will need to sell it in. No longer will you ask, "What do I sell?" Instead, you'll be busy wondering how you're going to find the time to sell all the product you see.

- To start out, sell everything you don't want anymore
- Take cues from the world around you
- Consider your own interests and markets you may already understand
- EXPERIMENT!
- Choose something readily available to you with an ensured profit margin
- Make sure your product is UPS-able
- Consider the Trading Assistant Program
- Buy inventory on eBay in wholesale lots
- Look into garage sales, flea markets, discount stores, and closeout sales
- Buy out of season, sell in season (or to different climates!)
- Become a broker—small businesses are teeming with product
- Try product sourcing

CHAPTER FOUR

Getting Started, Payment, and Shipping

Getting started on eBay is simple. To date, 115 million and counting have signed on, the tech-savvy and tech-phobic alike, grandmothers and grandsons, the couple down the street and the guy in the next cubicle. If you're already an eBay user, then you can testify to the relative ease of the process. eBay is about lowering the barriers of entry for Internet commerce. Howard, my father-in-law, had never used a computer in his life before he started selling his watches on eBay. Twelve months later, he has a thriving online watch business. My mother had never used a computer in her life, either, but she has quickly become an eBay expert. eBay, in fact, was her launchpad to the World Wide Web and computing in general. She can attach a file to an e-mail and upload an image while browsing an online news site, all while standing on one foot and juggling four tennis balls—almost. It can be a launchpad for you, too, if you're an Internet or computer novice.

Words of Wisdom

"Twenty-seven percent of eBay users are newcomers; they've begun to use the Net in the last twelve months."

—*Berrier Associates*

Sign-up

The very first step of your eBay journey is registering and getting a User ID. This can be done in less than five minutes. Simply go to ebay.com and click on the Register link at the top of the page.

You will be asked to enter identifying information and then to choose a User ID. Your User ID will become your eBay identity. Think about choosing a name that makes sense for your business and its future.

You may want to choose something related to the product you plan on selling. However, you may not want to do this if you plan on selling a variety of things. After all, one of the greatest benefits to running an eBay business is the ability to seamlessly switch your product line, so it can be useful to have a User ID that would work for just about anything. You can't go wrong by choosing something short, simple, and easy to remember. Look at Amazon. They don't specialize in rainforest artifacts, but it's a catchy name. So is eBay, I might add. When you are signing up your User ID, keep in mind that you are also

starting to build your brand. If you already have a User ID but are afraid that it won't work for your business, eBay will allow you to merge your existing account into a new account. It usually takes a couple of weeks for the merge to go through, but it's worth it if you started selling on eBay as BootyLicious77 and feel that might not be professional enough.

I work with a young woman who signed on to eBay about a year ago. She is married to a Frenchman and wanted her User ID to reflect her Francophile nature. She and her husband love to eat frog legs so she tried to use "frog eater" in French. It was taken, believe it or not, so she tried *grenouille*, which is the French word for "frog." That was taken, too. The young woman was born and raised in Poland, so she decided to flag her Polish pride instead and tried the Polish word for "frog eater." It was available, and today, her eBay fashion business, "Zabojad," is thriving. I'm not crediting her User ID for her success, but it doesn't hurt that people are intrigued by it. It is an attractive, mysterious word with an interesting ring to it. Your User ID doesn't have to be that dramatic, and it certainly wouldn't work for my business, but you can have fun with your choice. This is the era of Google and Yahoo!, so you have license to be creative.

Buy the Domain

There is one additional factor to consider when choosing an eBay User ID. It is likely that you will eventually want to create an outside Web site based on your eBay business—as I discuss briefly in the section on advanced techniques—so check to see if your user ID is available as a domain name on the Web. The easiest way to do this is visit highfivedomains.com. Right in the center of the page is a search field. Enter the User ID you're considering, and High Five Domains will show you if it's available as a URL, whether as a ".com," ".net," ".biz," and so on. If it is, you probably want to snatch it up while you can.

This is a very inexpensive thing to do. You will now have the basic branding elements in place to start your eBay business—your User ID and your claim to the appropriate address on the World Wide Web.

In chapter 7, I will discuss the possibility of hosting your own images. When you register your own Web address on High Five Domains or a similar service, they offer package deals that include Web hosting and other online business tools. I registered all my Ebay User IDs on eBay and then bought a domain name on High Five Domains. While I was there, I picked up adamginsberg.com as well. You may want to see if your name is available and reserve that domain while you're at it. You never know what you might want to use it for in the future. I, for one, had no clue at the time, but adamginsberg.com has become a very useful resource for former, current, and future eBay students of mine.

Become a Buyer First

Once you have registered, the first thing you should do on eBay is buy something.

Buy some office supplies, shipping boxes, a mousepad for your new business. Buy your husband or wife a little gift for letting you stay up late at night learning about eBay. Big or small, buy something. Most people start out on eBay as buyers. They hear about it from somewhere and think they ought to check it out. They start remembering all those toys they never got as children, which could be out there waiting for them on eBay. Maybe they'll find that rare limited-edition three-dimensional *Wizard of Oz* collector's plate. Once they get on eBay, a dozen other things they've wanted will come to mind. That's how it works.

I recommend buying first for a few reasons. The first is that this is a very simple way to familiarize yourself with eBay and the way it works. You'll learn how to navigate the site, conduct searches, and find the information you need. You'll be able to see how a variety of auctions are run and begin to get an idea of how to run your own. The second reason is just as key: to increase your feedback score.

It's good to experience eBay as a buyer, so you can

relate to your future customers. You'll know what they're looking for, hoping for, and expecting. You'll be able to observe the way sellers interact with you and what kind of customer service they provide. You'll see what a seller can do to really make your day, and what they can do to really turn you off. You can learn just as much from negative experiences on eBay as you can from positive ones, and you will inevitably be a better seller yourself having both of these under your belt. That said, if you don't have any experience yet with eBay, you'll soon find that the eBay community is comprised of honest, ethical people, and you will probably be impressed with what you discover. Once you start buying on eBay, it's hard not to make a long-term habit of it. Things you can buy elsewhere, things you can buy around the corner even, you will start buying on eBay. I buy everything I can on it. You can get great deals and support the community at the same time.

There is one more key reason why you want to consider buying first. eBay has a phenomenal mechanism called "feedback." Buyers and sellers are given the opportunity to rate each other based on individual transactions. Everyone has access to these comments. Your feedback is your reputation and credibility on eBay. When you start out with no feedback at all, it is difficult to get people to buy from you. They don't know yet whether they can trust you or not.

It all combines to create one rating. So buying on eBay provides a golden opportunity to begin paving the road to your new business by building up that vital element, your eBay reputation. Gathering feedback as a buyer is very simple. If you pay on time, you will receive

Quick Tip

There is no distinction on eBay between feedback you receive as a seller and feedback you receive as a buyer.

good feedback. Once you build your feedback as a buyer, people will trust you as a seller.

The magic feedback number on eBay is ten.

Once you have a feedback score of ten, I recommend that you start selling full-force. You can still list items and experiment as you're building your credibility, but ten is when you can really set your business in motion. There are additional benefits to getting ten feedback, which I will discuss throughout the book. Begin buying, play with listing a few auctions as well, and fly into action as soon as you reach that magic number.

Create a Seller's Account

Before you can start listing auctions on eBay, you have to create a seller's account. Although you need additional information, this process is just as simple as the initial registration. After entering your User ID and password, you will be required to provide both a credit card and bank account number. eBay uses this information only to verify your identity. They will not charge you and they will not share the information with anyone else. To ensure that eBay remains a safe place to do business, they make certain that every person selling on the site is exactly who they say they are. Providing as much peace of mind for buyers and sellers as possible is one of the pillars of eBay's success.

Once you've registered a User ID on eBay, there are just three simple steps you need to take to create a seller's account: the first step is to verify your registration information, the second step is to choose how you wish to pay your seller fees, and the third is to choose what form of payment you will accept from buyers. When you click on the "Sell" link on the eBay home page, if you are not already registered as a seller, eBay will prompt you to do so.

You will be asked to verify your information with eBay by putting either a credit card or debit card on file as well as your checking account information. Setting up the seller's account is free—this information is kept just as verification of your identity on eBay's secure servers.

Next, you will be prompted to choose how to pay your seller fees. eBay charges for every listing and every completed sale on the Web site. At the end of the month, they will either charge your credit card or debit your checking or PayPal account. I would encourage you to have them debit your checking account. As your eBay business grows, so will your seller's fees. I had months where our seller's fees sometimes exceeded $25,000 a month. My credit card does not have a $25,000 limit. If I had opted to have eBay charge my credit card for my seller's fees, the transaction would be declined almost every month. eBay will close down your account if your credit card is declined when they attempt to charge their fees. You can avoid this by opting for eBay to debit your checking account instead.

PayPal

The last step required in this process is choosing the methods of payment you will accept from buyers. On eBay, the preferred method by far is PayPal. Recently acquired by eBay, PayPal is an online payment system that allows people to send money to anyone with an e-mail address, using either the funds in their PayPal account, a confirmed bank account, or any major credit card. If you accept PayPal, you automatically accept Visa, MasterCard, American Express, and Discover. This is a groundbreaking system for small businesses. You no longer have to go through the complicated and expensive process of setting up a merchant account to be able to accept credit cards. Merchant accounts run a credit check and charge enrollment fees and high transaction fees to Internet users. Within fifteen minutes you can have a working account with PayPal and be open for business. They charge about 2.2 percent for accepting credit cards, which is very fair, considering your alternative. PayPal is an immediate, simple, and relatively inexpensive way of conducting online transactions.

Aside from the ease and cost, PayPal is safe. Essentially an online bank, they provide an excellent service. If you want to pay someone using your PayPal account, all you need is their e-mail address. You tell PayPal whom to send the money to, and they do the rest.

Because transactions are carried out only between two e-mail addresses, the seller's and the buyer's, there is no need to exchange sensitive information. You never have to give anyone your credit card number or even your PayPal account number.

PayPal is the only entity that sees this information during your transaction. Many eBayers will not purchase from a seller who doesn't take PayPal, because it is the only method of payment they are comfortable with. PayPal offers buyer protection, so if an item arrives damaged, or never arrives at all, they will be reimbursed.

Once again, peace of mind is essential to the success of any online business, and the eBay–PayPal dynamic duo is the ideal delivery platform for Internet commerce peace of mind. PayPal has fifty million members and counting all across the globe. It is so ubiquitous that PayPal is becoming a form of currency in and of itself. In the future, your PayPal account may well be the most important and possibly the only account you have.

You can PayPal money to any person for any reason.

If you have to collect money for your child's school fund-raiser, or a family trip, or an office gift, you can simply have everyone PayPal it to you. The word PayPal is now a verb.

Quick Tip

> Instead of wiring money to someone, you can simply e-mail it.

Move over, Western Union. Another benefit of PayPal: they have just introduced buyer financing, whereby buyers can make purchases on eBay and, through their PayPal account, pay over time. Sellers receive the payment in full at the time of purchase.

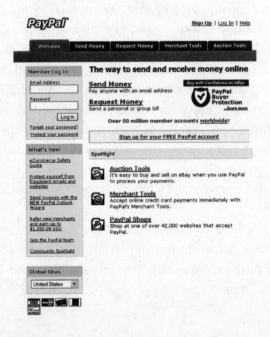

*Signing up on PayPal is easy. Just go to paypal.com, fol-
low the "Sign Up" link, and click on the Business Account
option to get started. Opening a business account as
opposed to a personal account will allow you to accept
credit card payments from your future customers.*

A year and a half after I started selling on eBay, I was
at a conference. At dinner I overheard a few of the people discussing how they get cash back from their PayPal
account. I had no idea what they were talking about, and
that infuriated me. PayPal offers a debit card, and it took
me a year and a half to find out about it. The minute I
got home after the conference, I got on my computer and
signed up for my debit account.

Fun Fact

You can apply for a PayPal debit card once you've been
registered with PayPal for sixty days or have been selling on eBay for six months.

As an incentive, you'll receive 1½ percent back on all
purchases made with that debit card.

PayPal can save you 50 percent on all your eBay fees!

PayPal fees themselves are less than three percent of
the transaction price, so the 1½ percent will make a serious dent in your already minimal overhead. Do your gro-

cery shopping, Christmas shopping, back-to-school shopping, all with your PayPal debit card. If you pay for as many business expenses as possible with your PayPal debit card, you can save a tremendous amount. My debit card arrived in the mail two weeks later, and I've been getting 1½ percent back ever since.

It's hard not to sing the praises of a system that has basically sealed the deal for the future growth and success of Internet commerce in general, and eBay in particular. Without it, people would be much less inclined to buy directly from another individual, as distinct from a large, established Internet presence.

PayPal has opened the door for folks like you and me to offer the same protection as Amazon, Barnes & Noble, or Circuit City.

Together, eBay and PayPal are revitalizing the small-business entrepreneurial workforce, returning the mom-and-pop idealism of our parents' generation to a lucrative reality for this generation and the next.

Getting Started

- Register and choose a User ID that could work for a business
- Consider buying the corresponding domain name on the Web
- BUY FIRST!
- Create a seller's account
- Sign up for your PayPal account
- Get your PayPal debit card when you qualify

Shipping and Handling

If you recall the story of my first pool-table auction, you'll remember that I had little faith that it would actually sell, so when it eventually did, I was left with my tail between my legs and a thousand-pound object to ship across the country. I had no idea how to accomplish that feat, but the winning bid had thrown me into the virtual water, so I had to gather my wits and come up with a plan. Pool tables ship in parts, which means that they have to be assembled wherever they're going to sit. So not only did I have to get the thing out to Farmingham, Massachusetts, but I had to make sure someone would build it wherever bodyshop44 intended to keep it. After culling my contacts on both coasts, I found a billiards shop near Farmingham that would assemble it and a freight company that would package the parts and send it over. bodyshop44 chose his felt color and, within a week, the pool table was on its way.

Luckily, most things people sell don't require all the effort called for when you're selling and shipping pool tables. However, shipping is still one of the biggest cost factors in running your business, and you need to develop a shipping strategy that will minimize your cost while maximizing the service you're providing to your customers.

Charge a Little More

There are a few different theories as to how to charge for shipping. Some people believe you should charge your buyer exactly what shipping will cost you. I believe it is an acceptable practice to profit a little on shipping. This doesn't mean that I charge outrageously. I don't charge $40 if the actual cost is $4. This is against eBay policy and will repel almost all, if not all, your buyers. I might, however, charge $6.95:

Quick Tip

I don't think of shipping as just shipping. I think of it as shipping, packaging, handling, and insurance.

I have to pay someone to wrap the item up, put it in a box, label it, and send it off. I have to buy bubble wrap, Styrofoam popcorn, packing tape, and a cardboard box. Even if you're working a one-person operation, there is a lot of time involved in seeing your packages off. The adage applies here—time is money. Every box you prepare is time you can't spend listing another item. In economics, the term is called "opportunity cost." This refers to the monetary value of a missed opportunity. If you're an hourly worker at Burger King and you burn your hand on the fryer, the cost of the accident is not just the amount on your medical bills, but the lost wages from the week you had to take off. When you're running an eBay business, the time you spend shipping will inevitably cut into the time you can spend listing. Factor all of these costs, both time and material, into your shipping fees.

You can also use shipping and handling to make up

for some of your eBay fees. When you list an item, there is a cost involved. When you boldface the item and add a gallery picture, there is a cost involved. When your item sells, a final-value fee is assessed. When you accept a PayPal payment, you're charged a percentage of the transaction. Granted, these costs are minimal for any particular listing, but taken together over the course of a month or a year, they certainly add up. This is the overhead of your eBay business. It's small, compared to that of the brick-and-mortar world, but it is there and it affects your bottom line.

Therefore, just as you would do for any traditional business, it makes business sense to cover your costs wherever you can. Just make sure you continually balance your cost-covering strategy with the value proposition you provide in the marketplace. No one will buy from you if the cost of your products outweighs the value they provide.

The $2–$3 extra I'm charging for shipping can help pay for the cost of doing business on eBay. Charging a fortune for shipping and handling is anathema to your business, but it is okay to build in margin to cover some of your overhead.

People often ask me why, for example, a customer would pay $12 shipping on a $7 purchase. This, again, comes down to a value proposition. If that same item costs $32 in a store, they will gladly pay you $19. If it costs $17 in a store, you may still sell the item, but only if it is harder to come by. eBayers understand that shipping and handling is part of doing business on the site.

As you start to experiment with products to sell on eBay, shipping costs will be an important factor in that process. Eventually, you will settle on products that you can acquire cheaply enough so that the combined price and shipping charge will lure bidders and still deliver the profit margins you are seeking.

Determine Your Shipping Cost

There are a few ways to charge for shipping. You can determine one flat rate and charge that to anyone anywhere in the country. When we do this, I pick the farthest possible place in the continental U.S. from where I am. My business is based in Southern California, so I use Florida as our standard. I determine what shipping will cost for a customer in Florida and then charge everyone in the country exactly the same. If I ship to Florida, I will break even, but if I ship to Arizona, I might make a few dollars. This saves the time and effort it would take to determine what shipping would cost for each location I have to ship to.

For customers outside of the continental U.S., I include a note in our listing to e-mail me for a shipping quote. There is no reason to worry about how much an item will cost to ship to Germany until you have a customer in Germany who may want to buy. The exception to this is if you're planning to specifically target an audience in a foreign country. I know a doctor who sells iPods solely to the eBay market in the United Kingdom in his free time. (How a doctor is managing to find free time is an entirely separate discussion.) Apparently, there is a high demand for them and, with it, a lucrative iPod price differential between the two countries. Of course, I've just blown his whole plan, since four thousand of you will start selling iPods to the United Kingdom, but once again, that is an entirely separate discussion. He has become familiar enough with shipping costs to areas all over that country that he can confidently state his international shipping charges to the United Kingdom in his listing.

Shipping Calculator

eBay has recently added a rather helpful feature called the "Shipping Calculator," which you can include in your listings. Using this tool gives you a quick and easy way of figuring out your shipping costs, and it's fun because it makes your buyers do some of the work for you. When you opt to include the shipping calculator in your listing, eBay will prompt you first to choose the method you will be using to ship. All UPS and U.S. Postal Service options are available to choose from. Then you will be asked to provide some size and weight information about the package you will be sending. If you wish to add an amount for handling on top of whatever the shipping cost turns out to be, it will allow you to do that, too. The final step is up to your potential buyers. When they view your listing, they can enter their zip code and find out exactly how much shipping and handling will cost them.

I generally ship via UPS Ground. Insurance is included.
They provide a very reliable service, and, most important,
they pick up your packages at your door. As your business
begins to grow, you'll appreciate this time-saving service
more and more.

Use eBay to Determine Your Shipping and Handling Fee

If you are still unsure as to what you should be charging for your shipping, use eBay to find out. Conduct a search to see what others are doing. My auctions generally have the most expensive shipping in every category I sell in. I'm constantly researching what my competition is charging to ship the same items I'm selling. I find out what they're charging, and then I charge just a little bit more. We do, however, provide an excellent service. Bidders can see this from our feedback and by the professional appearance of our listings, and the slight difference in shipping fees is worth it to them, because they feel comfortable buying from us.

Wow 'em!

There is a concept that I live by, which has become the foundation of my eBay business. You will hear it throughout the book. It can be said simply enough in two words:

---

underpromise, overdeliver

When you go to the Cheesecake Factory, the perky

out-of-work actress working nights as a hostess invariably tells you your wait will be forty-five minutes to an hour. When your little pager goes off in thirty minutes, you're thrilled. Now, if Bunny at the counter had told you twenty minutes, you'd be upset when your table finally opened up ten minutes after that. Same thirty minutes. Underpromise, overdeliver. We tell people their pool table will ship within five business days. It usually ships the same day it's paid for.

Adopt a Policy

It is a good idea to adopt a fairly consistent shipping policy. You will save yourself the time it would take to make item-by-item decisions. You can create a template for your shipping policy description to include in all your listings. Some items may require special handling or instructions, but you can usually use the same general parameters again and again. Occasionally, I offer free shipping and handling as a promotional tool to attract buyers to my auctions. This is a good strategy to employ once your business allows for it, and you might find that you're making enough profit per item to offer free shipping regularly. I will touch on this further when we explore listing strategies in chapter 5.

PayPal and UPS: Seamless Shipping

The most effective method for shipping is to utilize PayPal. PayPal integrates with eBay and UPS. Once you have created your UPS label through eBay, your customer automatically receives a tracking number. Shipping through PayPal is simple and a great time-saver. Gone are the days of manually entering buyer contact information and then sending tracking numbers. Here's the process:

1. Log into PayPal.

    You will see orders that have been paid for. You will also see a column titled "Action."

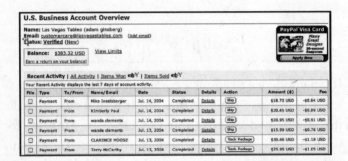

2. Click on "Ship" in the Action line.

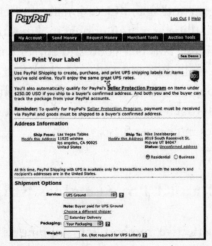

You will be taken to a "UPS—Print Your Label" page.

You will notice that the "ship from" and "ship to" address are all ready to create the shipping label. Simply select service (ground, overnight, etc.) and enter the dimensions of the item you are shipping. Your shipping cost will be calculated for you immediately. "Press Submit."

3. Print your label.

4. Call UPS—they will come right to your home and pick up the package. That's it. Simple, effective and huge time-saver, yet most people don't even know this method of shipping actually exists. And some who stumble upon it get confused by it.

Next time you log into PayPal, the action "Ship" will be replaced with "Track Package," so you'll know what and where you have and have not shipped. And all the tracking information is stored in there, in case you need to access it.

International Shipping

Another element to consider in your shipping strategy is where you are willing to ship your products to. This decision has broader implications that should be closely aligned with your overall business strategy. You can limit your shipping to any specific areas you choose, or you can ship worldwide. I only ship our pool tables in the United States, because of their size and the prohibitive expense involved in international freight transportation. On the other hand, Howard has shipped watches to over thirty countries around the world. Sometimes, you don't even have to ship at all. If you're selling your old refrigerator, you can say, "Will not ship, local pick-up only."

When you select "worldwide" as your shipping option, your listing is automatically placed in every eBay country in the world.

With a click of a button, you are open for business everywhere in the world where there is Internet access.

Awaiting you are 115 million customers. If your item allows for it, I recommend shipping worldwide. The eBay platform hands you the unique opportunity to become an international business overnight. Your business can benefit from different values placed on the same item by people in different parts of the world. There is no need to limit the potential of your business unless you have a strategy that targets a specific location, or your item is inherently difficult to send overseas.

If you do decide to ship internationally, there are a couple of additional factors to consider. For one, many countries charge import duties and taxes on incoming goods, based on their declared value. As a seller, you are not involved in this process at all and have no idea what buyers will be charged. I disclose this fact in my listings. An international buyer will usually know that they are responsible for these import charges, but as you will later see, every single aspect of the transaction that might result in a questionable situation after the winning bid has been made should be explicitly stated in your listing. Sometimes, these duties can be rather steep. For example, a buyer in England may be required to pay as much as $50 or $60 on a $300 watch. This is definitely something they have to take into consideration when making their purchases. Because of this expense, many buyers will ask if a seller is willing to list the item as a gift of low monetary value on the customs declaration form. Some sellers are happy to comply, because they feel it increases their chances of making a sale.

There is a risk in agreeing to do this. You can only insure an item for the amount you declare it to be. If I send a $300 watch but list its value at $25, I can only get $25 coverage in insurance. If something happens to the item during shipment, if it is lost or damaged, there is nothing that can be done about it. I will only get a $25 check for a $300 watch. In our shipping policy, it is clearly stated that I will not mark an item as gift or declare its value to be worth any less than it actually is. We let people know in advance exactly where we stand. This may result in a few lost international sales, but nothing is risked and the integrity of the business is maintained. Taxes are a fact of life. We all have to pay them. It may not be worth the risk to pacify a few international buyers.

Organize your shipping! If you are running your eBay business out of your home, you can make shipping an easy and efficient process by setting up a little mailroom area near your workspace. Get a postage scale that can handle larger packages (you can buy it on eBay!). You'll find that a scale will save you time and allow you to accurately gauge your shipping costs, and it will pay for itself in no time. Organize all the supplies in your "mailroom" and create an assembly line for yourself. Ship a group of items at once to save time.

My mother has elevated shipping to an art form. She has a stockroom that used to be my sister's bedroom. All her Beanie Babies are divided into individual bins, with one Beanie Baby sitting on top of each, telling Mom which ones are inside. She has all her packing material perfectly organized, and she goes down the line, preparing all of her shipments at once. Then my father comes home from his medical practice to sign in for his second job. He's my mother's mailman. Dutifully, he takes her packages and ships them off while she starts the process

Shipping and Handling

- Charge a little—but not a lot—extra to cover handling and insurance
- Consider the "value proposition"—will the shipping cost together with the price of your item still be a value for buyers?
- Decide between charging a flat rate or using the Shipping Calculator
- Use UPS Ground
- Use eBay as a research tool to decide what to charge
- UNDERPROMISE AND OVERDELIVER!
- Adopt a policy you can apply to most of your items
- If it's feasible, opt to ship worldwide
- Organize your shipping

all over again by listing new items. It's a great system if you can get your family to sign up for it. Shipping is a big part of any online business. Approaching it in a simplified, systematic way can have a significant positive impact on your bottom line.

CHAPTER FIVE

Policies and Listing Strategies

Policies

About three months after I started selling on eBay, I came home one Sunday after lunch with my family to check my auctions. *They were all gone.* Every one of my auctions had mysteriously been removed. This was my first introduction to the fact that eBay has policies. Before that day, I had no idea there were rules on eBay. I thought eBay was like the World Wide Wild West before the sheriff came to town, and pretty much anything goes. I learned the hard way. I changed my listings to conform to the policy I had broken only to see them all come down again. eBay would send me an e-mail telling me which policy I had violated, and I would fix the offending element. Then my auctions would get canceled again. This kept happening. People became irate. I was running pool-table auctions that started at a penny with no reserve and free shipping. The final prices would end up somewhere between $1,900 and $2,300. There was an extraordinary amount of bidding activity, and buyers were emotionally invested in the process. Sometimes the auctions would disappear fifteen minutes before they were supposed to end. I started getting hate mail. "If you didn't want to sell your pool table, why did you list it in the first place?" That was one of the nicer ones.

I started putting a banner at the top of my listings. It was a disclaimer that read, "If your auction ends early, it is eBay who is shutting it down. I have no idea why." Luckily for me, one of eBay's attorneys happened to be looking for a pool table. He saw my banner and sent a very nice e-mail, in which he wrote, "I think I may be able to help you. I don't know what the trouble is that you're having, but I'll be happy to help you craft your auctions and work through all of this with you." Working with this lawyer really opened my eyes to the fact that eBay is not a game. It is a big business. I didn't know they had rules and I didn't know they had lawyers. They have all of that and more. They have attorneys and legal protections and policies in place to protect the community. eBay does everything it can to create a safe environment for both buyer and seller. It is as secure as any marketplace can be in which transactioneers never meet each other face-to-face.

This attorney was kind enough to explain to me everything I was doing wrong. Since he contacted me, I have not violated one rule. My listings have stayed put. I did, however, waste a lot of time, energy, and heartache learning that eBay has policies, and this is not a necessary roadblock. If you learn the rules in the beginning, you can avoid this sort of problem and start out ten steps ahead of where I did.

---

eBay does not monitor its listings. The community polices itself. Unless you are reported, eBay will not know of, or do anything about, the violations you commit. It is the responsibility of the members of the community to watch one another.

A Good Samaritan saw that I was breaking eBay policies and reported me. If you catch someone else doing so, you should do the same. eBay will remove the offending auction and send a warning to the seller. This may sound like being a tattletale, but the strength and integrity of the community remains in the hands of its members. Knowing the rules is helpful to everyone in the eBay community—both you and your competitors. One of the amazing things about eBay is that it presents a level playing field. It is everyone's responsibility to make sure that it continues to do so.

Quick Tip

The rules are the same for a first-time seller, a corporation, a small-business owner, and a Titanium Power-Seller.

This is what makes it possible for you to start selling tonight and immediately compete with anyone on any level. That is definitely something worth protecting.

Choice Listings

The first policy I violated is called "choice listings." When you list something on eBay, you are listing one item. You are not allowed to give choices. You can't list a pair of shoes and offer the buyer a selection of sizes. If you want to sell multiple sizes, you have to run a separate auction for each size pair you have available. If you want to sell an iPod mini, you can't let the buyer choose from the colors you have in stock. You must list your green iPod mini, your pink iPod mini, and your blue iPod mini as three distinct auctions. From eBay's standpoint, you are avoiding listing fees by offering multiple items under the guise of a choice for the buyer. This posed a unique problem for me as a pool-table vendor. We offer nine different felt colors. I was supposed to list nine separate auctions so eBay could make nine separate listing fees. Pool tables, however, are a different animal from most items. They don't initially come with felt. Pool tables arrive in pieces and the felt is customizable. If you buy a new pool table anywhere in the world, you will get to customize your felt. I explained my dilemma to eBay, and they allowed me to continue offering a color of felt as a customizable option at the close of the listing.

The same is true of our diamond rings. Our product is not really the ring itself but the stone. Therefore, we don't offer five different ring sizes and settings of the same stone. If you buy the stone, you get to customize the size and setting of the accompanying ring. Most items, however, are not the exception. If you're selling T-shirts in small, medium, and large, you are required to list them in three different auctions.

Fee Circumvention

The most frequently committed offense on eBay is referred to as "fee circumvention." Fee circumvention is when you provide someone with the opportunity to purchase something outside of eBay. eBay makes a commission—final-value fee, as it is called—from every item sold on the site. If I offer to sell my item to a buyer directly, eBay loses their commission. They put me in touch with the buyer but make no money for the service they've provided me. To stay in business, eBay cannot allow fee circumvention.

Offers to sell items outside of eBay come in many different forms. Some people do it directly in their auction listing. Someone may be selling a bedroom set, for example. They'll sell a headboard, footboard, dresser, mirror, and one nightstand. Then, in the listing, they'll include a note that says, "Second nightstand available, $200." Any person buying a complete bedroom set is going to want two nightstands. The seller is trying to make a little extra money by avoiding paying the commission on the extra nightstand they know they will sell. This is a clear violation of the fee-circumvention policy.

In the body of your listing, you are not allowed to include any links to third-party Web sites. This is another example of attempting to sell items to eBay members outside of eBay. If I include a link to my Web site, where I'm selling all the same items as in my auctions, what I'm doing is stealing eBay's customers. Even if you are not selling anything on your Web site, you cannot provide a link to it. eBay does not allow you to use their Web site as an advertisement for your own.

Without knowing it, I flagrantly broke this policy. I wasn't selling anything on my third-party Web site, so I wasn't trying to circumvent eBay's fees. I was simply providing a link to more information about the product being offered. As I said, this is still against policy. When eBay pulled my auctions and informed me of the policy, I removed the link. I still, however, included the URL to my Web site. It just wasn't clickable. They call this a "static URL." I finally read all the policies, but they're confusing. When I looked through the material, I had no idea what a static URL was. My listings were removed again, so I instead put a caption under my images that read, "Photo courtesy of lasvegastables.com." None of this is allowed. I wasn't trying to break the rules, I just didn't understand what was and wasn't permitted. The only exception to this rule is in your "About Me" page. I will discuss this feature at length in chapter 11, but the "About Me" page is a free mini–Web site eBay hosts, providing you an opportunity to tell the community a little bit about yourself. You may include a link to your third-party Web site in your "About Me" page.

Another form of fee circumvention is ending an auction early if you decide you don't want to sell the item. Imagine, I list a pair of earrings worth $200. I've seen similar items sell for that amount, so I start the bidding at a penny with no reserve. One hour before the auction is to end, the bidding is only at forty dollars. I don't want to lose my investment, so I end the auction early. I have denied eBay its percentage of the forty dollars I would have sold the earrings for. You may end an auction early for extenuating circumstances. If, for example, you are selling a vase and your cat jumps up and knocks it over, smashing it to little pieces, before the auction ends, eBay will allow you to remove the listing.

Along the same lines, you cannot refuse to accept payment or refuse to deliver an item once an auction has ended. Just as bidders are required to buy, sellers are required to sell. This may seem obvious, but there will always be people who try to get out of an unfavorable situation. If you are a nonselling seller, as eBay calls it, you may get suspended temporarily or indefinitely. It is much better to take one loss than to risk your entire eBay business.

Charging outrageous shipping fees is another form of fee circumvention. When eBay got started, this was not the case. People did this all the time. For example, someone might be selling a $500 digital camera that costs $10 to ship. In their auction, they would sell the camera for $15 and then charge $495 for shipping. eBay doesn't make a commission on shipping charges, so the seller would be able to pay eBay as if they had sold a $15 camera instead of a $500 one. The buyer didn't care, because it was all the same to them. Realizing this, eBay changed the rules and now you can only charge reasonable shipping and handling fees. Any activity designed to create sales outside of eBay, or to prevent a sale from occurring, is fee circumvention and is not allowed.

Keyword Spamming

There are some policies I managed to avoid violating. One of these is called "keyword spamming." Misleading titles and keywords are not allowed. For example, there is a very popular designer brand of women's clothing called Juicy Couture. Many people sell it on eBay and many people search for it on eBay. Someone may put "Juicy Couture–like" in the title of their listing, knowing that anyone searching for Juicy Couture will see their listing. This is not permitted. It is unfair competition for the people who are actually selling Juicy Couture and misleading for buyers who are conducting their search for the perfect pair of sweatpants. I didn't break this rule, because a pool table is a pool table. No one out there is really searching for a designer brand.

Payment Surcharges

Another practice not permitted on eBay is "payment surcharges." Unless you say so in your listing, you cannot charge a customer additional funds for choosing to pay with a credit card or PayPal. This is against not only eBay's policy but also that of Visa/MasterCard. I do not recommend trying to get around this.

Never bid on your own items. Never have someone you know bid on your items in an attempt to drive up the price. This is called "shill bidding," and not only is it against eBay policy, it is also a felony. If you have an item selling well below its value, you may be tempted to call a friend and have them bid a little so you don't lose your shirt. You may get away with this once or twice, but it is not worth the risk. eBay has protections in place to detect these practices, and you may find yourself banned from the Web site for life. eBay has a number of rules and regulations, and if you are unsure about a practice, feel free to review their policies listed right on the site.

Listing Strategies

Now that we know the rules of the game we're playing, it's time to start listing our items. eBay has kindly made

Policies

- Learn the rules on eBay
- Practices to avoid:
  - Choice listings
  - Fee circumvention
  - Keyword spamming
  - Payment surcharges
  - Shill bidding

the actual listing of an item a very simple process. They have created what they call a "Sell My Item" form. It takes you step by step through the listing process, laying out everything in an extremely user-friendly manner. eBay itself has tutorials in case you have any problems, but this is unlikely. Because listing an item is self-explanatory, in this chapter I will instead address the philosophies and strategies involved in doing so.

eBay Fees

First, it is important to understand how eBay makes their money. Knowing the fees you will be charged allows you to make informed decisions regarding some of the concepts discussed in this chapter. There are two main fees involved with any auction listed on eBay.

Fun Fact

Whether your item sells or not, you will be charged a listing fee. This fee varies depending on the minimum bid you set. These prices currently range from $0.30 for the least expensive item to $4.80 for the most expensive.

These prices are subject to change, however, so I recommend checking eBay for current details.

If your item sells, you are charged a final-value fee, or a commission, which is usually a small percentage of the final price of the auction. If your item does not sell, there is no final-value fee to pay. The exception to this is if you are selling cars on eBay Motors, where there is a flat $45 fee to list the car and a flat $45 fee when it sells. eBay Real Estate is also unique in that they offer a flat listing fee starting at $150 for thirty days. There is no final-value fee for real estate sold on eBay.

Compared to other Web sites and to advertising you'd have to pay with a retail business, eBay fees are very fair. Between eBay and PayPal, you will generally pay about 7 or 8 percent of your final value in fees. Amazon charges 15 percent. Recently I had the opportunity to teach an eBay seminar in Fort Lauderdale. A one-day full-page ad in the local Fort Lauderdale newspaper, Sunday edition, with a circulation of 360,000 will cost you approximately $29,000. On eBay, you can list an item for $0.30 and reach an audience 115 million strong. eBay provides phenomenal opportunity and an invaluable service. Without the infrastructure and selling platform eBay presents, we couldn't be in business in the first place. Their fees are not outrageous, and they allow room for great profit. They are very careful to make sure that both you and they can profit from sales. I consider eBay my partner, and I definitely want to do my part to keep them in business.

Listing Format

When filling out your "Sell My Item" form, you will first be asked to select a listing format. There are two main formats to choose from. The first is the traditional auction format, where you set a starting price, bidding ensues, and the high bidder at the end of the auction wins the right to purchase your item at the price of their final bid. The second is the fixed-price format, in which there is no bidding at all. If you want to sell your rare Dan Marino rookie card for $50, you list it for $50, and if someone wants to buy it at that price, they do. If you have only one, the first buyer who clicks to purchase wins the right to buy. The auction ends and your listing disappears. If you have multiples of your item, your listing will remain until all the items have sold or the auction ends.

Fixed-price

For someone starting out on eBay, I generally recommend using the traditional auction format. As your feedback and business grow, there are, however, significant benefits to making use of the fixed-price format. It is ideal if you are selling multiples of the same item. Imagine you have twenty-five of those rookie cards. You could sell them one by one, auctioning one off every three days and then listing another as soon as it sells. It will take you two and a half months to sell all of them. With the fixed-price option, you can list them all at once in the same auction and sell them as quickly as people will buy them. Remember that eBay charges a listing fee for every auction you run on its site. Listing those twenty-five cards over the next two and a half months will cost you twenty-five individual listing fees. No matter how many items you include in your one fixed-price listing, you pay only one listing fee. That's an incredible savings.

Buyers often like the fixed-price option, too. They can purchase the item immediately instead of waiting three days for the auction to close, and they know they get to purchase. For some buyers, this format lacks the excitement, urgency, and opportunity for a really great deal that are the hallmarks of a traditional auction. Many others, however, don't need those things. They don't like the uncertainty and the hassle. They just want to find their item, buy it, and move on with their lives.

There is one final advantage to the fixed-price format. The majority of the bidding in eBay auctions occurs in the final hours and minutes before the end of each auction. There are two reasons for this. The first is that people want to wait until the end to try to get the best price possible. The second is much more practical. Auctions on eBay are listed in order of those ending soonest.

Quick Tip

Your item reaches the top of the list only when the auction is almost over. This is when the highest number of people see it and this is when they are most likely to buy.

A fixed-price auction can end at any time because of its very nature, but it still has to wait until toward the end of its close to reach the top of the list. When your fixed-price listing finally gets to that stage, you may sell more than just one. In those last few hours you may sell three or four or five, because people can finally see them. This is when you get the most amount of traffic. People will see and they will buy. Once they buy, however, the auction doesn't disappear. You don't have to wait three days for one item to reach the top of the page. You can have as many as you want and sell to anyone and everyone looking for your item until you're out of stock.

Buy It Now

A nice combination of the auction and fixed-price formats is a new feature eBay has created, called "Buy It Now." This allows you to set a fixed price within the auction format. You take your Dan Marino rookie card and list it with a starting price of $1. You then set a Buy It Now price at $50. If someone takes this option, the auction ends immediately. However, if a bid is placed before a buyer chooses Buy It Now, the option disappears. This gives buyers an opportunity to do one of two things. They can bid and hope that by the time the auction ends the price of that football card will be less than $50. If the Buy It Now disappears, there is a chance that the bidding will go higher than the original "Buy It Now" price. On the other hand, they can buy the card for the $50, ending the auction and ensuring that the item will be theirs.

For a seller, there is an additional benefit to taking advantage of the Buy It Now option in your auction format. You can use it as a tool to set the perceived value of your item.

Listing your rookie card with a Buy It Now price of $50 immediately tells potential bidders that that is what it's worth. You can set the Buy It Now price at higher than the actual value of the item. If your rookie card has a Buy It Now of $75, some buyer may think they're getting the deal of the century when they get it for the $50 you were hoping for all along.

Choose Your Category

Let's assume you have chosen the auction format to sell your rookie card. The next step is to select your category and subcategories. There are twenty-seven thousand categories on eBay. It is very important to choose the appropriate category for your item. If you don't, there is a chance a potential buyer searching for exactly your item won't be able to find it. In searching for the right category, think from the viewpoint of the buyer. If you were searching for your item, what category would you look in?

If you are still uncertain as to the category your item belongs in, use eBay as a research tool and conduct a search yourself. There are two ways to find the proper category. eBay itself has a tool on the "Sell My Item" page to help you. You will see a line that says, "Enter item keyword to find category." Punch in your keywords— Dan Marino rookie card—and eBay will give you suggestions as to what category your item belongs in. You can also do the research yourself. Look for your item, or one like it, and see what category others have listed it in.

Sometimes your item will fit well in more than one category. As I stated earlier, eBay charges a listing price for each item you sell. It is important to know that if you choose to list your item in more than one category, you will have to pay a listing fee for each additional category. Unless your item really does fall into two very different categories, you may want to pick the more obvious one and stick with it. If there are two strong categories for your item, do a completed-item search. See which category produced more successful sales. If they are equal, it does not matter which one you list in. If not, choose the one that seems to yield more bids.

After choosing your main category, you then search within that category to find the proper subcategory. The main category for your rookie card is "Sports Cards and Memorabilia." The first subcategory you would choose is "Cards." In the end, the exact category your card belongs in is Sports Cards and Memorabilia > Cards > Football-NFL > Rookies (1980–89). Your item now has an eBay home.

Pricing Strategies

There are a few theories on how to price your item for your auction. The first is to set the number at the minimum you are willing to sell it for. If you would be sick to your stomach selling your rookie card for anything less than $40, you can set the price there and hope that it sells. If no one buys it, you haven't lost anything. If they do, you at least get the minimum you were looking for. This is a very safe option with minimal risk.

Another option is to start the bidding for your auction at $0.99. eBay charges listing fees based on the minimum price you set for your item. The higher your minimum price, the higher your listing fee will be. Items priced $0.99 and under pay the lowest listing fee. The first increase occurs at a dollar. It is a good idea to always look at where price increases occur. If your minimum bid is just above one of the cutoffs, you can save money by changing it to just below the cutoff.

Human psychology plays a part in pricing strategies. In our consumer world, online or in a shopping mall, we often come across items we absolutely must have. We may not have even known of the item's existence, but once we see it, we feel we can't live without it. We will stop at nothing to get it.

On eBay, as soon as we bid on something, there tends to be an immediate psychological transfer of ownership.

We may not have won the item yet, but just the act of bidding seems to make us think it is already ours. If you bid on an item at even a dollar, you begin to think of it as yours. The two hours and twenty-six minutes left in the auction is all that stands between you and your property. Then someone else outbids you. They have taken from you what is yours. You must take it back. Even if you don't want it anymore. It is a matter of principle. The dreaded outbid notice arrives in your e-mail with the news that someone has taken your item. You may end up bidding more than you ever would have spent just to hold on to what is rightfully yours.

Psychology drives up the price of auctions. Items starting at a dollar can actually yield higher prices than those with a high minimum bid.

Someone may click on your Marino card auction. They have no intention of spending the $50 you want, but they'd gladly take a shot and bid a dollar. Then, when they get outbid, they'll bid $5, $10, and $15. By the time the auction price reaches $50, they're so emotionally invested they'll gladly bid $55 in order to win. This is a real phenomenon that will make a difference in your bottom line.

Another good time to start your auction at $0.99 is when you aren't sure of the value of your item. Perhaps you find an old vase in your house. You can't find one like it in your eBay search and you have no idea where it came from. Since you have nothing to lose, list it for $0.99. You may sell it for $0.99, but you may also find you have a valuable collectible on your hands. You had no idea what you had, and you may end up selling it for more than you had hoped. When there is nothing to risk, this is a fun game to play.

A friend of mine goes to garage sales to find his product. He recently found an old piece of crystal he thought was interesting. He paid $5 for it. He knows nothing about crystal and had no idea what it was worth. When he searched for a piece like it on eBay, he couldn't find anything. He wanted to put a $20 fixed price on it. He figured that $20 gross for a $5 investment was an excellent profit. Since he really had nothing to risk, he decided to start it at his $5 investment and see what would happen. It turns out the piece of crystal was a rare collectible. Although it was slightly damaged, the final price of the auction was $221.

The ultimate decision as to whether to start your bidding at $0.99 or a higher minimum bid should be based on the demand there is for your item. If there is a high demand, there will be a lot of bidding activity. Starting your auction at a low price may drive up the price. If your item is rare and there are only a few people out there looking for it, there may not be enough bidding to create a fair price. Then you may want to consider a higher minimum bid.

Consider the demand for your item and price it accordingly. When I started out on eBay, I can remember an experience my cousin had. She sold a small stuffed pig from the movie Babe. *It was signed by the actress who did the voice of Babe and was a rather rare collectible. Thinking people might get excited about this little pig, Robyn listed it for $0.99. She didn't think about the fact that there aren't that many Babe memorabilia collectors out there. A very excited woman won the auction at the opening bid and paid less than a dollar. She sent Robyn an e-mail telling her that she was an avid Babe collector. This piece would be the jewel in her collection's crown. Robyn realized that this buyer would have gladly paid much more than $0.99 and that she should have started this auction with a much higher opening bid.*

Reserve Auctions

There is one final pricing option eBay provides you. You may list your item at a low starting price with a hidden reserve. This means that you do not sell your item unless the bidding reaches the secret reserve price. If you list that rookie card for $1, but include a reserve of $40, you don't actually sell the card unless someone bids $40. eBay charges you 1 percent of your reserve price for taking advantage of this option but will refund it to you if your reserve is met. The reason they do this is because many people were using the reserves to avoid eBay final-value fees. In addition to listing fees, eBay charges a small percentage when your auction is successful. If your item doesn't sell, you don't have to pay a final-value fee. People used to set incredibly high reserves, knowing that bidders would never reach the price and the item wouldn't sell. When the auction ended unsuccessfully, they would e-mail the high bidder and offer them the item at the price of their highest bid, thus avoiding the final-value fee. This is an obvious case of fee circumvention and is not allowed in eBay policy. eBay figured it out fairly quickly, however, and began charging a percentage of the reserve price to discourage people from the practice.

I do not recommend using reserves for one key reason. Buyers don't like them. They don't like not knowing the true price of an item and how far they are from being able to purchase it. There is no transfer of ownership if the reserve hasn't been met, because the buyer knows they have not bid high enough yet to buy the item. Often, buyers will e-mail the seller, asking outright for the value of the secret reserve. Many sellers don't like answering that question. If I were selling using a reserve, I would gladly answer that question every time. If they know the price of the reserve, they may jump at the chance to bid it just so they know they will actually be able to win the auction. As long as you are not using outrageous reserves, there is no reason to hide this information from serious customers.

Fun Fact

> Statistically, no-reserve auctions yield higher prices than reserve auctions.

Many buyers will not bid on reserve auctions at all. They simply don't want to deal with worrying about what that price is, and they are convinced that whatever it is, they won't be able to get a bargain. eBay is all about the bargain. No-reserve auctions, especially those with low starting bids, create a great deal of excitement. I mentioned earlier that most of the bidding in eBay auctions occurs in the last few hours or minutes before the auction closes. This is especially true for auctions with no reserve. Buyers want to buy as cheaply as possible, so they wait until the end to bid to avoid driving up the final price. They hope to be able to jump in at the last possible moment, snatching up the item for almost nothing. Often, in our no-reserve auctions we start the bidding at a penny and then sit back and watch what happens. We do it with $300 watches and we do it with $2,000 pool tables. This may sound terribly risky, but contrary to conventional wisdom, prices will end higher in no-reserve auctions, where there are no limits, than in those with a reserve.

In life, as on eBay, when people are not confined or limited, they tend to do more.

On eBay, when people start bidding on something, they don't simply want it—in their mind it is already theirs. That outbid notice is like a declaration of war. They will fight like warrior kings to protect their property.

I was speaking to a woman about an auction she lost. She was bidding on a $25 bottle of perfume. She walked away from the auction in the last five minutes because she thought it was in the bag. In the end, she was outbid by $0.50. She was incredibly upset by this outcome. She was so emotionally invested in this $25 item, readily available at any local mall, that when she was speaking to me two days later, I could still hear the frustration in her voice. I believe she would have paid a lot more than she would have at the mall just to have been the winner. The item itself loses importance. Winning becomes all that matters.

A few years ago, a study was conducted on this very topic. The question was whether reserve auctions made more or less money than no-reserve auctions. To create a completely level playing field, the minimum bid of the no-reserve auctions was equal to the secret reserve price of the reserve auctions. A test was devised, in which fifty pairs of identical collectible cards were listed for auction separately on eBay. One card would be listed with a very low minimum bid and a secret reserve. The other, absolutely identical card would be listed with a minimum bid equal to the secret reserve placed on its twin. For example, within one identical set, one card may have a minimum bid of $0.01 with a secret reserve price of $10. The other card would have no reserve, but its minimum bid would be set at $10. In the end, 72 percent of the cards with no reserve ended up selling, while only 52 percent of the ones with reserves did. Of the cards that did sell, the ones with no reserve sold on average for $0.62 more than the ones with reserves. Buyers simply hate not knowing where they stand.

I encourage people to use no-reserve auctions and low starting bids. It makes your heart beat. I have had so much fun watching auctions that looked in the last few hours like a total loss. Then, all of a sudden, a bidding war starts and in the end the price was even higher than I'd hoped. I can't guarantee this will happen. Sometimes you may lose, but with no-reserve auctions, you tend to make more money overall than you lose in one or two individual auctions. People simply do more when they are free from boundaries or limits.

No-reserve auctions can also be valuable advertising tools. Often you will see a retail store advertising a deal so good that it can't possibly be profitable for them. They do this to create traffic, to bring people into their store, and to get them to look at the other items they have for sale. You can use no-reserve auctions in the same way. People may come for the $0.01 no-reserve auction and then stay to check out all the other auctions you have listed. One auction like this can significantly increase the exposure for your twenty-five other auctions that all have more reasonable minimum bids. When you put a reserve on things, you tend to get fewer bids, and the auctions, over a period of time, will end up closing for less. You will make more money with no-reserve auctions than you will if you use reserves.

Buy It Now Strategies

There are separate pricing strategies for Buy It Now auctions. I discussed earlier how you can use the Buy It Now price to create a perceived value for your item. That is one strategy you can employ. Another idea is to set the minimum bid close to the Buy It Now price. Let's say your rookie card has a minimum price of $40 and a Buy It Now of $50. A buyer will probably pay the Buy It Now price instead of risking losing the item for a mere $10 less.

I may have discouraged you from using reserve auctions, but there are certain circumstances in which you might want to experiment with them in combination with the Buy It Now option. I stated earlier that a Buy It Now option disappears when the first bid is made. This is not true in a reserve auction. In a reserve auction, the Buy It Now option does not disappear until the secret reserve is met. If you have a Buy It Now of $50, start the bidding at $1, but create a reserve of $40, you have no more risk than if you set the minimum bid at $50. You do not sell your item for less than $40, and the Buy It Now does not disappear until that price is met. When the minimum bid and the Buy It Now price are close together, there is very little bidding. Usually someone decides to buy the item or they don't. Buyers will not have the same fear of the secret reserve price, because they know what the Buy It Now price is and know that the reserve will be set somewhere below that. Because buyers feel free to bid, you have the opportunity to create that sense of ownership I discussed earlier. Someone who would never bid $40 might bid $16, get caught up in the moment, and spend more than they ever planned. Even with a reserve, you may end up with a bidding war on your hands. The final value might reach and exceed not only your secret reserve but also your Buy It Now price.

Auction Length

After setting a starting price, you next decide on the length of your auction. eBay offers you a choice between one, three, five, seven, and ten days. It is a good idea to list very rare items for ten days. This allows the few people out there who may be searching for an item like yours enough time to find it. Otherwise, I generally recommend three-day auctions for almost everything. You want to make the most of those last few hours of bidding. The longer your auction lasts, the longer you have to wait until the end, when your auction is finally at the top of the page. Often, people search in order of newest listings instead of those ending soonest. They look for certain things on eBay, they search all the time, they know what's out there, and they just want to know what's new. The three-day auction gives you one day as a new listing, one middle day, where nothing much happens, and one final day, where most of the action occurs.

There seems to be no difference in final prices when you look at the length of an auction. Unless, as I stated, your item is very rare, it will garner the same amount of money regardless of the duration of the auction.

Therefore, shorter auctions allow you to sell faster, and if you have multiple items to sell, you will make more money.

Recently, eBay has added the one-day auction as an additional option for ID-Verified sellers with a feedback rating of at least ten. Thousands of people sell concert, sporting, and other event tickets on eBay. Often, people don't get tickets to sell until shortly before the event. They get sick and can't go, or someone gives them a few extras. Whatever the reason, people were unable to sell them on eBay because the shortest auction was three days. Recognizing that some auctions are time-sensitive, eBay introduced the one-day option. Regardless of the item you are selling, one-day auctions are a valuable tool that can increase your sales and profitability. The faster you sell, the more money you can make. Now, instead of selling an item every three days, you can sell one every day. Many people ask why you wouldn't just list more than one item using the three-day auction. You could list your item every day, so that you have an auction ending every day of the week, selling as many items as you would with a one-day auction but allowing people a little more time to find your wares. The problem with this is that your auctions will overlap.

If you have two or more of the exact same item listed at once, there is no urgency on the part of the buyer.

They know there are multiples of the item available and have no need to jump at the chance to buy. In a one-day auction, only one is listed, and the auction is ending today. This creates a great sense of urgency.

I do not recommend using a reserve in one-day auctions. If your item doesn't sell, you have to pay the 1 percent reserve fee. If you relist it multiple times, those reserve fees can add up. Do a no-reserve and include a Buy It Now if you so desire. There are no one-day auctions for the fixed-price format, so Buy It Now is the only

---

eBay Fun Fact—Think Outside the Box Office

Each week, enough tickets are sold on eBay to fill the Louisiana Superdome. With high sales prices and amazing sell-through rates, selling tickets is easy, profitable, and 100 percent legal. Take advantage of the features that have been specifically designed to make eBay the premier marketplace for event tickets. Most tickets are purchased with the Buy It Now feature.

way to offer a similar feature. eBay loves a one-day auction. It increases their listing fees, because people are able to run more auctions. You sell more and they make more on the fees. It's a win-win situation. Experiment with one-day auctions. I have found that they work better with some items than others. If the item you're selling is something a lot of people are looking for, it will work very well in the one-day auction format.

Freebies

I like to offer freebies in my listings. This strategy provides an excellent advertising tool. I state boldly in our pool-table auctions that every buyer will receive all of their accessories for free. If you buy a pool-table from LasVegasTables, the purchase will include—for free—your rack, cue sticks, balls, chalk, etc. I make sure to include the fact that this is a $500 value. We all love getting something for free. My wife is the queen of freebies. At LasVegasTables, we make special offers on a large, grandiose scale. My wife does it in her own way. If she sells a purse, she includes free makeup samples she received at Macy's. If she sells a shirt, she throws in a matching barrette. I don't think I've ever seen her list an auction without some freebie listed as bonus. If you're selling a camera, offer a free carrying case and some film. If you're selling a printer, throw in some ink cartridges. When I was in direct sales, we would call this a "first-call special." Give people an incentive to buy from you, and give them an incentive to buy now. You don't typically see freebies on eBay, and this is one more way to set yourself apart from the crowd.

Timing Is Everything—or Is It?

The last element to consider in listing your auction is timing. Many people want to know when they should list their auctions. There is a concern that if an auction ends at the wrong time, people won't see it and the price will be lower than it should or the item won't sell at all. The truth is, there is no wrong time. eBay is a twenty-four-hour, seven-days-a-week juggernaut. There are always people buying. There may be better times than others, but once you establish a business and are selling many items at once, it doesn't matter at all when you list. It is best to have auctions closing all the time. Some people refrain from listing on holidays. I sell a couple of pool tables on Christmas Day every single year. People may be looking for somewhere to spend the money their grandmother gave them as soon as the ham and fruitcake are gone. Sales are made on eBay every single day of the year.

Empirical data tells us that the best time to list a Citizen watch is between six and eight o'clock on Sunday night. I may be selling two hundred watches at a time. They can't all end Sunday evening at seven-thirty. I want my auctions closing around the clock every day of the week. This gives all kinds of people opportunity to find my product. They may work the night shift, they may live in Australia, and they may be a struggling actor who tends bar nights and weekends but is almost always on the Internet on weekday afternoons. I want to give each and every one of them a chance to buy a watch from me. If you are still in the hobby stage and selling your treasures one by one, you may want to consider listing in prime time, so your auctions end when the largest number of people are searching.

If you're running a high-volume business and selling as a major source of income, you don't have to worry about when an individual listing is ending.

You can make more money and maximize your business potential if you list a number of items all the time.

Words of Wisdom

"Fall seven times, stand up eight."   —Japanese proverb

Strategies for All Seasons—Try Them All!

I discussed a number of different listing strategies in this chapter. There is no one particular strategy I recommend. I would never tell you, "List your item in this format, at this price, for this many days." Experiment with all of these things.

It's important to keep in mind that factors such as season may affect your strategy. At Christmas time, fixed-price or Buy It Now auctions may work better than traditional auctions. People want to click the button and have the item shipped to their recipient. They want to get their shopping done and they don't want to waste their time playing around, bidding, and waiting for auctions to end. List some items with no reserve, and some with a Buy It Now. List some with a reserve and a Buy It Now. List some with a minimum bid of $40 and a Buy It Now of $50, and yet others with a Buy It Now of $75. List some items with a fixed price. Try three-day auctions and one-day auctions.

Experimenting allows you to monitor the pulse of your business. The more you experiment, the more you will be able to see what works and what doesn't work for you and your product.

Listing Strategies

- Choose a format:
  - Traditional auction
  - Fixed-price
  - Traditional auction with Buy It Now
- Choose your category and subcategories
  - If you are unsure, use eBay as your research tool
- Use the supply and demand of your item to determine the starting price
- Avoid reserves except in combination with a Buy It Now option
- Run three-day auctions for most items
- If your item is very rare, run a ten-day auction to maximize exposure
- One-day auctions are good for high-demand items you have multiples of
- Throw in some freebies
- Don't worry about timing if you sell enough items
- Experiment with all these strategies and see what works best for your items and your business

Part Three

Power and Velocity

CHAPTER SIX

Titles and Descriptions

The buzz phrase and foundation of the real estate world is just as crucial on eBay as it is in the peddling of land: location, location, location. Here, instead of waterfront property, it refers to your item title. You are given fifty-five characters to work with. Those fifty-five characters are the most valuable real estate you have on eBay.

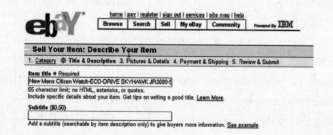

Titles

Think like a Shopper

Your title, made up of keywords, is what brings customers to your listings. It's how they find you. Whether your product is in high demand is less important than whether or not the 115 million and counting eBay members can find it. They can't bid on it if they can't find it. This makes your choice of keywords one of the most crucial elements of your eBay business.

When you are thinking about what keywords to choose to maximize your item's chances of being found by a potential buyer, it's important that you put yourself in the buyer's mind. Imagine you are looking for the item you want to sell. What words will you use to describe what it is you're trying to find on eBay? Break it down even further and think first about which keywords you would search if it was that exact item you were looking for, and then think about what you would type in if you were looking for something similar to your item. There's always the possibility, after all, that a potential bidder might be looking for something like your item, but not exactly. Once they see it, though, there might not be any turning back. They must have it.

There are two ways on eBay for people to conduct searches for items they want to buy. With the first, they look in the category and subcategories in which they want to browse. You collect Happy Meal toys, so once a day, every day, you check the Toys & Hobbies, Fast Food,

Cereal Premiums: Fast Food: McDonalds category to see if anything new and really exciting has turned up. We discussed this earlier, when we talked about the importance of choosing the right category.

The second way is the more common way eBay searches are conducted. Just like Google or Yahoo!, eBay has a search engine. It works the exact same way the other search engines do. You type in the keyword(s) you're looking for, press Search, and eBay does the rest. You don't want just any fast-food giveaway, you want the set of four Burger King Return of the Jedi drinking glasses you used to have when you were eleven and your mother gave to Goodwill when you were sixteen. So you type in seven words—return of the jedi burger king glass—and you're thrilled when two pages of listings appear in your browser. Some seller had a Burger King glass to sell, so they put it in the title. You were looking for a Burger King glass, so you entered that into the search engine. eBay did a little matchmaking and brought you both together. Your title is the main way people can find you and is therefore a critical component of your success.

Think like a buyer. Imagine trying to find your item. What words would you type in and search for? It's important to put yourself into the mindset of the buyer and then match your keywords as closely as possible to what you think they might type in to find your product.

One of the best ways to find keywords for your title is to use eBay once again as your valuable research tool. Have a look around. Search for your item, or one as similar as possible if you're selling something unique. Test a few different possibilities and see which ones yield the most results. Almost everything there is to sell is already being sold on eBay. There's no need to reinvent the wheel.

"Key" Keywords

There are a few basic elements that identify your item, which you typically want to include, if applicable. The first is *brand name*. I'm not selling any old camera, I'm selling a Canon. It's important to be as specific as possible. At any one time, there may be two thousand listings for "Canon Camera." Adding a *model name* to your title—Canon EOS Digital Rebel, for example—narrows down the competition considerably. Sometimes you may even want to include a *model number* to further differentiate your item, depending on whether the model number is an important identifying feature, and on how many keyword spaces you want to use up.

Another element to consider is your item's *condition*. Indicate whether what you are selling is new or used. People will often search for "used" items if they are looking for a price bargain, and they will search for "new" if that is important to them. By putting this in your title, you are further targeting your potential bidders. The year is sometimes an important detail. It certainly is if you're selling a car. Also, people often search for words like "antique" or "vintage." This is when "used" becomes desirable again and actually increases the perceived value of what you're selling. Color and size can also be critical.

If your item is a limited edition, you may want to include that, if you have space for it. Try to make room in your fifty-five spaces for any identifying detail you think people might search for.

Quick Tip

Identify exactly what it is you're selling and maximize your item's possible search hits, so you don't get lost in the crowd.

Sometimes we don't even realize some of the details people are looking for. For instance, a lot of eBayers like to search for their name, just to see if anything comes up. If you're selling a picture, a sign, a vintage T-shirt—anything that has a name or a place on it—include that in your title. An old photograph of Vinnie's Bait Shop may just be exactly what Vinnie is looking for. Someone desperately homesick for McGehee, Arkansas, the little town they grew up in, might be out there buying up anything and everything they find with the word "McGehee" on it. Mark Stevens might come upon the "Vintage Mark Stevens' Auto Shop T-shirt" and pay top dollar for it in all the excitement from seeing his name on a shirt. However, if your listing merely says "Auto Shop Vintage T-shirt," Mark might never find it, and your shirt will probably end up selling for less. The simple fact that the item you're selling exists means there's someone out there who wants it. Use your keywords to help them find you.

Key Keywords for Your Titles

1. Brand name
2. Model name
3. Model number
4. Condition
5. "Antique" or "vintage," if applicable
6. Color
7. Size
8. Any distinguishing or personalized features to help buyers find your item

Keyword No-No's

While there are a number of things you want to include in your titles, there are also a few things to avoid. We don't want to waste our valuable real estate. Try not to use words like "gorgeous" or "stunning." If someone wants to buy a watch, they might type in the brand or model or type they want. They might punch in "ladies pink watch diamonds," but I doubt very seriously they're going to punch in "gorgeous watch." I have done a lot of searching on eBay. There are great deals to be had, and, more often than not, I buy what I can there instead of in retail stores. I have spent hours and hours conducting searches. I have never searched for "stunning," ever. In two and a half years, I've never searched for "gorgeous." I've never searched for "amazing." I don't think anyone else has, either. Still, sellers constantly use these words in their titles. They think it will entice people to click on their listing once they've found it. If they made better use of that real estate, however, more people might find them, driving up both the number of bidders and the final selling prices of their auctions.

You will often see sellers using different symbols—$, @, !, &—in their titles in another misguided attempt to draw attention to their listing. The problem is that nobody searches for symbols, so they're squandering characters on things that don't bring people to their auctions. There is a word I constantly see in eBay titles—"L @ @ K." Sellers think this makes their listing stand out. Again, no one is searching for "L @ @ K," so it's a waste of four characters.

I always see the phrase "brand new" in titles. "New" is important, but I'm less certain about "brand." For some people, there is a difference between "new" and "brand new." For others, there isn't. It's entirely subjective. There is no objective definition of "brand new." When zWatches sells a watch on eBay, it comes directly from the manufacturer, in the box. It has never been opened. Most people would agree that's "brand new." Before we ship it to you, however, we open the box and inspect the watch, making sure that it works and is in perfect condition. I think that's still "brand new." I'm not sure what it would be called if I'd never opened the box but had left it sitting in my house for six months. Even if you have your own notions about the difference between "new" and "brand new," most people don't search the word "brand" when they're looking for "new." Use the great expanse of space in the description to explain exactly how new your item is. For the title, I recommend abandoning "brand" and simply using "new."

Another thing to avoid is abbreviations buyers would not search for. I recently saw a listing for basketball tickets. The title read: "Los Angeles Lakers Basketball Front Row Tix." The seller ran out of room, so they abbreviated "tickets." The problem is that "tickets" is probably the most important word in that title, and few people hoping to score some decent seats for the playoffs are going to search using the word "tix." In this example, it might be smarter to abbreviate "Los Angeles," since "LA LAKERS" is something someone might search for.

Useful Abbreviations

There are a number of abbreviations that are OK and actually desirable to use. These words and phrases are so common in titles that the eBay community has agreed to use shortcuts, freeing up room for more detail. The most common of these abbreviations on eBay is "NR." If you have no reserve in your auction, use the letters "NR" in your title. Most eBayers know what this means. In addition, eBay has a tool called "Smart Search" to help you in this area. If someone searches for "No Reserve," any listing with "NR" will appear. I have occasionally encountered new eBay users who are unfamiliar with this abbreviation. Just recently, I had a diamond listed with no reserve and, as always, had "NR" in the title. I received an e-mail from a potential bidder asking if "NR" meant

"Not Real." Don't be afraid to use it, though, because people learn quickly. Another accepted abbreviation is "FS." If you're offering free shipping, you want to say so in your title, because that's something people get excited about. You probably don't want to waste thirteen characters on "Free Shipping," though, so "FS" is a huge space-saver.

Spell It "Rite"

When it comes to titles, spelling is critical. I once advised a woman who constantly misspelled words in her titles. She was selling an expensive, trendy, and hard-to-find polka-dot dress. In her title, she spelled it "p-o-k-a." She couldn't understand why no one bid on her item. I explained to her that in all likelihood no one saw it to bid on, because anyone looking for a polka-dot dress was using the letter "l" in their searches.

On the other hand, I tell buyers to type in common misspellings of the item they're looking for, because if they do, in fact, find that item misspelled, they'll probably be the only ones who do. It's a great way to find bargains on eBay.

If you spell your words correctly, you'll let someone else be the provider of those great steals.

Grammar? Who Cares?

While spelling is crucial in titles, grammar is completely irrelevant, contrary to what Mr. Boyle might have taught you in the sixth grade. Simply use the block of words that people are going to search for. They won't be punching in sentences, so you don't have to, either. Once we get to the body of the listing, we'll be more concerned about grammar. For now, all we care about is that the necessary keywords are present.

Quick Tip

Not only is punctuation irrelevant, but it is a waste of real estate and can actually work against you.

People don't normally use punctuation when they are typing in keywords. If you have a period or a comma or some other punctuation mark right after a word, your listing won't appear unless someone searching places the same mark in the same place.

Quick Tip

The only punctuation mark you may want to consider using is the apostrophe, if you think someone might use it in their keyword search.

In some of our watch auctions, the apostrophe in "Men's" is used, and in others, it is not, because it seems that about half the people type it into their searches and half don't. A buyer searching for the Gilligan's Island bath toy they had when they were a kid will probably use an apostrophe in their search. If you're unsure as to whether you should include it, search eBay and see what other sellers are doing with the same item. You can also use both versions if you happen to have extra characters to spare.

Use Spaces

It is also important to separate your keywords with spaces. Some sellers will use the word "*freeship*," putting an asterisk to the left and an asterisk to the right, with no space in between the two words. And yet, when you type in "free shipping," and people do search for "free shipping," it won't come up, because there's no space in between. Separate your keywords and remove the asterisks and people will find you.

Item Specifics

"Item Specifics" is a new tool eBay has recently implemented. It is not yet available in every category, but soon it will be. It allows a seller to categorize their item specifically and a buyer to find exactly what it is they're looking for. If you are searching for a digital camera, for example, you can narrow down your search as to type, brand, resolution, or megapixels, and condition. For every category, the options offered are different and relevant to the items therein. The clothing category wouldn't ask about megapixels, but certainly color and size. This is a great tool to make use of if it's offered in your item's category. It's simply one more way to make sure your listings are showing up on computer monitors far and wide.

Choosing a Title

- Think like a buyer
- If you're not sure what keywords to use, conduct a search for your item
- Don't use symbols like * and @, or uncommon abbreviations
- Use "sanctioned" abbreviations, like NR and FS, to save valuable real estate
- Double- and triple-check your spelling
- Remeber that searches are not case-sensitive
- Grammar doesn't matter
- Use spaces
- Fill out "Item Specifics" form, if available

Descriptions

The fifty-five characters of the title limit us. They force us to choose our words carefully, abandon grammar, and ignore those eye-catching adjectives we're just dying to use.

All of that changes when you write your description.

You have an entire page of space to wax poetic and give your item the attention and consideration it deserves. Along with your photographs, the description you write is the way you tell your buyer exactly what they can expect from your item. This is the only information they have to base their purchasing decision on. Therefore, it is a good idea to be as comprehensive and detailed as possible.

Just as you did earlier with the title, you want to put yourself in the mindset of the buyer as you're writing your description. Try to think of any questions they might have regarding your item and beat them to the punch by including that information. The more detailed your description, the better off you are. In chapter 7, we'll discuss telling a visual story with your images. Here, you want to paint a picture with your words.

Reiterate and elaborate on all the details you included in your title. Product type, brand, model, color, size, condition, and age are all important to include. It's often helpful to use bullet points, so that your listing is easy to read. Your description is the place to delve into exactly what you mean by "brand new." I recently won a DVD player at a raffle. I took it out of the box, looked at it, and decided to sell it on eBay. Putting everything back was like a jigsaw puzzle, and I simply couldn't get it to look as it had when I first opened it. The parts were out of the box for maybe five minutes, but I wasn't sure how they had ever fit inside. I couldn't even close the top properly. In my title, I used the word "new." In my description, I wrote, "Opened, inspected, never used." They'll now understand why it doesn't look as it should if they had just brought it home from Circuit City.

Quick Tip

> You will have happy, satisfied customers if your items arrive exactly as described.

We've all had experiences where we've ordered something in a restaurant or bought something from a catalogue and it was "not as described." When it happens to me, I don't usually bestow repeat business on that establishment. Try to be as accurate as possible. Outline all the features and benefits. Include anything that distinguishes, your item from others like it. If it comes from a smoke-free home, say so. This matters to a lot of buyers. Measure your item and list the dimensions.

Tell 'em What's Bad, Too

Be sure to include flaws in your descriptions. Mention any dents or scratches. If something doesn't work properly, say so. This advice might seem to go against your better judgment at first. After all, how often do you walk into a store, even a second-hand store, and hear the salesperson tout all the wonderful defects of the merchandise you're interested in? The salesmanship philosophy on eBay in this regard is very different from that at the brick-and-mortar. A bidder's mentality on eBay is geared toward trusting that they don't have to see and touch an item to know very clearly what they're bidding on. You'll become a successful seller on eBay by solidifying that trust over time.

If you choose not to mention an obvious imperfection because you're afraid the item won't sell—say, the silver paint on the back of your used Handspring Visor PDA is partially chipped—you run the serious risk of getting a negative feedback from a buyer who was expecting a Handspring that looked new.

By fully describing all the features of your Handspring—good, bad, and ugly—you are ensuring that when your high bidder receives their item, they will be thrilled with it. Remember, there are many people out there who want your product even with its imperfections. I sold my old radar detector. It was broken, it had no power adaptor, no manual, and no warranty. It was three years old. I made all of this very clear in the auction description. Someone bought it. They had one like it at home, with a broken part, so they bought mine for the spare parts. When it arrived, it was just as I said, broken, no power adaptor, no warranty. They were as excited about it as a kid walking into Disney World for the first time.

Clearly describe the pictures as shown. If there are any discrepancies between your photo and the item, outline them. The color might be a little different. Perhaps a scratch is too small to be seen in the image. I will go into this further in chapter 7, but you might want to use the phrase "Not Actual Size" for any item that might be misconstrued by the buyer as the size of the picture. My wife bought a change purse. The listing made no mention of size, and the picture seemed to depict an average-sized change purse. She didn't think to ask the seller for dimensions. When it arrived, it was tiny. She may have been able to fit two quarters inside. Disclose all of this information. Again, measure your item and give exact dimensions to avoid this problem entirely.

Make 'em Want It

You will get a lot of window shoppers. The counter at the bottom of your listing telling you how many visitors you've had will be a lot higher than your actual number of bids. Use wording to motivate those window shoppers to actually bid. This is basic marketing, no different from strategies you'd use if you had a brick-and-mortar store. You want to give them a reason and a desire to take action and bid on your auctions. Create urgency. You want people to feel like if they don't bid now, they are going to miss out on a great opportunity. Phrases like "Limited Time Offer," "Special Price," and "Close-out" are motivators. Hard-to-find items are in high demand on eBay. Words like "rare," "unique," and "one-of-a-kind" encourage people to buy. Use "you" and "your" to create the feeling of ownership in the buyer. "This vase will look beautiful in your home." If the bidder begins to think of it as theirs, they will fight for the chance to buy it.

Count Your Visitors

It is very easy to include a counter like the one I just mentioned in your listing.

When you reach the bottom of step 3 of the "Sell My Item" form, "Enter Picture & Item Details," you will be presented with page-counter options.

Having a counter will allow you to see the number of page hits your listing gets. You can choose to display a counter, you can opt for a hidden counter if you don't want potential bidders to see the number of hits you've had, or you can decide to have no counter at all. I recommend always including one, because the information it provides it valuable. You can see how much traffic you're generating and what percentage of that traffic is moved enough by your listing to bid. You can use this information to guide your listing strategies as you discover what brings visitors to your auctions and what doesn't.

eBay presents you with a link to andale.com, the service that creates and provides the counters. If you visit Andale, you can sign up for free and choose from a wide variety of counter styles to further personalize your listings. Andale provides a number of additional services to eBay sellers, including hourly and daily hits reports, which give you in-depth analyses of your listed items. They also allow you to do bid comparisons on other items in your categories, so you can see how you match up to your competition. It is a valuable site to check out and take advantage of. They will help you sharpen your listing strategies and improve your bottom line.

Special Offers

Imagine you've just gotten hold of an entire case of Harry Potter Lego sets for less than wholesale. You don't have the room to store them and you want to sell them quickly. One idea might be to include something like "Limited Time Offer. 15% Less Than Usual." Mention the retail price of the item, if there is one. This helps create a perceived value for the item. If you're offering those Legos at 50 percent less than retail, people will get excited.

Tell a Tale

Quick Tip

If there is a great story involving your item, consider telling it in your description.

A piece in the news recently caught my eye. A guy was selling his ex-wife's wedding dress on eBay. He personally wore the dress in the photograph. His description was hilarious. He tells this whole story about how he found the dress in his attic and was going to burn it until his sister convinced him to sell it on eBay. His father-in-law never paid him back for the dress, but, still, all he really wanted out of the sale was enough for some baseball tickets and a couple of beers. It went on and on. He didn't have to spill his guts like this. He could have described the dress, included the size and the designer and the color, and left it at that, but he didn't. Apparently, people who saw the auction started forwarding it to their friends. It spread like wildfire, enough to garner media attention. The guy appeared on the *Today Show*. He wanted maybe a few hundred dollars for a $1,500 dress. The final price of the auction was $3,850. He also got five marriage proposals out of it. Every item you sell certainly won't have a story like that, but if it does, it couldn't hurt to include it.

List Your Policies

After you've described your item as accurately and with as much detail as possible, include all of your selling policies. Whereas your description of details is item-specific, you may be able to use the same selling policies in most of your auctions. These policies include shipping, payment, warranty, and return. State how quickly you ship and the method of that shipment, whether it is UPS Ground, U.S. Priority Mail, or one of the other many options available. As I discussed in chapter 4, remember to underpromise and overdeliver, so give yourself a cushion. If you think you will ship in three days, say a week. Include a price for shipping, or eBay's shipping calculator, so buyers know exactly how much money this will cost them.

Another thing we discussed earlier is the importance of having an international shipping policy. State upfront whether you are willing to write "gift" on the box or not. The buyer will want to know if they are going to have to pay tariffs, and this may make a difference in their decision-making process. If you are offering free shipping, don't just put "FS" in the title. Display that information prominently in the body of your listing. It is a powerful selling tool and you definitely want to exploit it.

I recently won an auction. I live in Los Angeles and that's where the item was. The shipping policy in the listing consisted of one sentence, "Call seller for shipping quote." I didn't call, because I intended on picking the item up. I wouldn't have bid on it otherwise. The price was great, and it was waiting for me a short fifteen-minute drive from my office. The reason the item had been so inexpensive, it turned out, was that the seller made up the money in their high shipping prices, which you didn't find out until you called them for a quote. I called them and said I was right around the corner and wanted to pick the item up. They told me I couldn't, that pick-up was not an option. If I wanted to pick up the item myself, I would have to pay an additional two hundred dollars. I argued the point. There was no mention in the item description that pick-up was not available. They argued back that it also didn't say that it was available. Aside from poor customer service, this was a textbook example of a seller failing to include his policies in his listing, thus creating both confusion and animosity in the buyer. It is critical to disclose everything. The smallest issue can change the perception of your business. I left the appropriate feedback, and now the same seller's listings include the phrase "No customer pick-up." If that phrase was there when I was looking, I wouldn't have bought it in the first place.

Here's an opposite example. My wife came to me furious after she had bid successfully on an auction. In her excitement over the item, she had forgotten to check the seller's payment policy. "I can't believe they don't take PayPal. They want me to go to the bank and get a money order. I'm so angry," she said. I asked her if this no-PayPal policy was clearly outlined in the description. She admitted that it was, but she hadn't seen it until the auction was over. I couldn't share her anger, because the information had been right there in black and white, for my wife to see.

State whether you accept PayPal, which automatically means that you accept Visa, MasterCard, American Express, and Discover. Let your buyers know what other forms of payment you will accept.

Most sellers will take money orders and cashier's checks, because they are very safe. If you accept personal checks but wait to ship until they clear, say that as well. If you are charging sales tax to residents of the state you're selling from, include it in your policy. Not everyone realizes that this is a law, and if you try to charge them sales tax when your listing didn't mention it, your customer may get upset. Be clear, specific, and comprehensive.

It is also important to include a return policy.

You may not want to accept returns, so you decide to say "All Sales Final" in your policy. Unfortunately, buyers don't like this. They see "All Sales Final" and they wonder if there's something wrong with the item. They think the seller is afraid that once the buyer receives the item, they will immediately want to return it for some previously undisclosed reason. In my research, I have found statistically that sales increase with a more tolerant return policy. If you're selling a broken radar detector, however, you may wonder how you can possibly allow returns. We've developed a policy that successfully solves both problems. The return policy we include in our descriptions reads, "All Sales Final Unless Not as Described." If the item is not as described, we will return your money in full. This inspires confidence in the buyer. There is no risk for them. They are going to receive the item you describe or they are going to get their money back. They feel comfortable bidding now. This allows us to satisfy people without taking returns, because we always accurately describe our items.

If you decide to include a phone number for inquiries, display that in your listing as well. When I first started selling on eBay, I signed up for an 800 number. Most sellers don't take phone calls. They don't want to be bothered. The reason they started an Internet business was so they wouldn't have to deal with people in person or on the phone. I find this to be a mistake. I will discuss this further in chapter 8, but the more you talk to people on the phone, the more you're going to sell. Every chance you get to explain your product, tout its benefits, and create a relationship with a customer will help your business. You will have the opportunity to ask them questions, to involve yourself in their world. Once you have a feel for their world, you can tell them exactly how your product will fit inside it. This is something you just can't do through e-mail. You'll be amazed by how much repeat business you get from people you talk to on the phone. They feel like they know you, like they can trust you. They become comfortable with you and they will not only come back time and again, they will tell their friends about you. A toll-free number may cost $30 or $40 a month, but the increase it will create in customer satisfaction is immeasurable.

Anticipate Questions

Your policy section is an important place to anticipate questions. You may actually increase sales by including more information in your descriptions. You're still selling that Canon Digital Rebel. A buyer looks at the auction and wants to buy it as a gift. It's Sunday afternoon, your auction ends in an hour, and they need the camera for a birthday party Thursday night. They e-mail you to find out if you offer rush shipping, because they can't find that information anywhere in your description. You're not at your computer. It's Sunday afternoon. You're at the beach with your family, where you belong. This is why you started an eBay business in the first place—so you could spend more time doing the things you love. The auction ends, and this buyer goes elsewhere, because you didn't get back to them in time. If you had anticipated the question and included it in your shipping policy, you would have made the sale and still gotten that tan.

Taking this theory to the next level, with the volume I deal with, I find it indispensable to include a

"Frequently Asked Questions" section. This can become an extremely valuable element of your descriptions and ultimately your business. "Frequently Asked Questions" is where you can ask and answer questions about your item and your policies. If you can imagine a buyer asking it, include it. It is amazing how much time and work this will save you as your business expands. The more you can anticipate, the less e-mail you will have to answer. Much of this you will learn as you go. I learned what questions people ask by, well, what questions people asked. In the beginning, I hadn't figured much of this out yet, and I would omit certain pieces of information. Then I'd get an e-mail asking me a question. I was happy to answer it. The second or third person would e-mail me, and I'd still be happy to send a response. By the eighth, ninth, or tenth e-mail asking the same exact question, a light would go off in my head. Maybe this is a frequently asked question. I'd know I omitted a key piece of information and I'd include it from then on. It's a simple learning curve.

A "Frequently Asked Questions" section is an important thing to think about when you're taking your eBay activities from hobby to serious business pursuit. If you're selling a few things from the back of your garage, you may have a couple of listings up at one time and you may get two or three questions.

When you're building your eBay business and using it to replace your current income, you may have fifty, a hundred, two hundred auctions all listed at the same time. With that many listings, you could have thousands of

customers looking at and bidding on your auctions.
Thousands of customers can generate a lot of questions.

If you anticipate most of those questions, you will save yourself hours and hours of answering e-mails. It will make your life easier and can even improve your bottom line, as in the Sunday afternoon example.

Grammar? Now We Care . . .

The last thing you want to do when writing your descriptions is forget to

---

proofread

---

for grammatical and spelling errors. While spelling is critical in the keywords of your title, it is still important in the body of your listing. Searches look for keywords in descriptions as well as titles, so sellers should make sure that all their spelling is correct. If you do some searching, you'll be amazed at the number of sellers who have poor grammar and misspelled words in their descriptions. In addition to being unprofessional, this does not inspire confidence on the part of the buyer. If there are enough errors, the buyer may consider bidding elsewhere. Remember, the words in a title are geared toward the keyword searches that buyers will input, but the words in a description are your only sales message to interested buyers once they have entered your corner of this vast virtual marketplace. You want to make sure that those customers who are looking to buy will be convinced that your item is the one they want to buy and you are the seller they want to buy it from.

Descriptions

- Keep thinking like a buyer
- Anticipate questions
- Paint a picture with your words
- Include and elaborate on details in your title
- Describe your item accurately
- Include flaws
- Describe photos as shown
- Create a sense of urgency with words like "rare" and "limited time offer"
- Include an Andale counter
- If your item has a great story, tell it
- List your policies—shipping, payment, warranty, and return   .
- Include a phone number
- Include an FAQ section
- Check spelling and grammar

Stand Out

At an additional cost, eBay offers a selection of features to make your title stand out. Of these, there are two I definitely recommend making use of. The rest may not be worth the extra expense if you're not selling a big-ticket item. No matter what your product is, the gallery option can help improve your sales. When you conduct a search, some of the titles will have a thumbnail photograph of the item just to the left of the keywords. The rest will simply have a symbol of a camera, indicating that there is a photograph included in the listing. Sellers including the tiny picture made use of the gallery option.

Gallery photo: the best $0.25 you can spend on eBay.

For the price of a mini York peppermint pattie at the counter of your local diner, your buyer can see your item without even having to click on your listing. Many sellers don't pay the extra quarter, and many buyers won't check out an auction unless that gallery picture is there. People like a sneak preview. It's an enticement, and when you're scanning a page full of search results, it becomes a crucial attention-grabber. Gallery will drive up your traffic and put you ahead of your competition.

The other option I'd advise taking advantage of is boldfacing your title's font. For an extra dollar, the words in your title will appear in bold, as opposed to the standard font. For an extra dollar, your listing immediately stands out from the crowd and encourages people to choose you from the fray. But before you take the "bold" option, research your item. Most sellers don't make use of "bold," but for some reason there are a few categories where everyone seems to do so. Then you make yourself stand out by not spending the dollar. In most cases, however, both "bold" and "gallery" are valuable selling tools.

Quick Tip

Build the $1.25 into your shipping and handling costs, and the customer will help pay for your advertising.

Make It Pretty

In our modern world, there are a number of selling environments. Everywhere you go people are trying to sell something. There are minimalls, lemonade stands, one-on-one presentations, and vendors selling fake Rolexes and Louis Vuitton handbags on the streets of New York. Compared to these, Internet businesses lack the human interaction. When a customer walks into a store, he can talk to the salesman, hear his tone of voice, and read his body language. He knows immediately if he likes and trusts this person who wants his credit card number. Unless they happen to call you with a question, you are just a User ID and an e-mail address to most of your customers. The only sales pitch you get to make is what you put in your listing. Just like when they're walking in and appraising a live salesman, buyers on eBay decide in an instant how they feel about your listing. As soon as they click, they know if they feel comfortable in your selling environment. They know if there is any chance at all of them bidding on your auction. The power of presentation on eBay is a rather important element.

The look of a standard eBay listing is not incredibly appealing. If you upload your photo and enter your description, you can let eBay do the rest. Your description will look like a block of text and your photograph will appear directly below that. This format can be hard to read, confusing, and not all that attractive, to boot. As they say, you get only one chance to make a first impression. If a buyer sees your listing and it appears dense and forbidding, they're going to shop elsewhere.

As you set up your listing, eBay will automatically present you with a number of options available to help you improve upon the basic listing. If you opt to use the "listing designer," then, for a nominal fee, you can choose from a wide variety of graphic themes for your listing. Each theme has its own colors, background, and borders to add to your plain listing. For almost any product you are selling, there is a theme available that makes sense. For your Canon Digital Rebel, for example, there is a border that places your entire listing in the center of a frame of film. There are also two "consumer electronics" themes and a number of simple shapes and colors. A broad range of options await you. After selecting a theme, you find a choice of layouts. Instead of featuring a big block of text and a photograph, the listing designer allows you to lay out your information in a manner that is both easier to read and more appealing. This tool is really useful to those starting out. It is simple to use, inexpensive, and makes a huge difference in the look of your listing.

When I started selling on eBay, I had no idea how to create a listing beyond plugging the necessary information in and pressing Send. As I did my research and looked around at other auctions, I realized just how much the look of the listing matters. Examining the competition, I

*decided that I wanted my listings to be fancy, sophisticat-
ed, and distinct from anyone else's. I had absolutely no
idea how to go about doing this. I wanted to stand out
from the crowd, to distinguish myself, but I didn't know
how. One option, I was told, was to learn HTML and
design my listings myself. "HTML" sounded to me like
something they would do on Star Trek to make the
Enterprise ship go faster. It was certainly not a term I was
familiar with. HTML, I quickly learned, is the code that
programmers use to create Web pages and Web sites. If
you are advanced enough or inclined to learn, you can
use HTML very successfully in your auctions. Many people
are sophisticated enough to use it. I am not one of them.*

In the beginning, I borrowed the HTML my mother
had slaved over for her Beanie Baby listings. Mom had
never used a computer in her life before she started on
eBay, but she had managed to teach herself HTML. It
took her three weeks of long hours and late nights. As
impressed as I was with her, I didn't want to go the same
route. I borrowed the fruit of her labors instead. She got
me into this whole thing in the first place, so it was the
least she could do for me. I pulled out her Beanie Baby,
along with all her frou-frou Beanie Baby colors, and
replaced it with my pool table. It was not the clean, professional, high-tech look I was hoping for. I wanted to
look like a serious company. Even though my business at
this point consisted of me and my computer in my basement, I wanted to create the perception that I was a big
corporation with offices and employees and Herman
Miller Aeron chairs. I ended up looking more like some-

one who had switched from selling Beanie Babies to pool tables last Tuesday.

Unhappy with that result, I hired graphic designers and spent thousands of dollars on high-quality listings. I found a Web company whose work I admired, told them what I wanted, and they created the HTML for me. In essence, each of my auctions was now a sophisticated, custom-designed Web site. You can do this, but it's incredibly expensive. For someone just starting out, I don't necessarily recommend such a costly investment.

zTemplates

The listing designer is useful, but everyone has access to the same themes, so it's hard to set yourself apart. HTML is difficult to learn. Hiring Web designers is cost-prohibitive. It occurred to me that there must be another option. Recognizing this need in the eBay community, I worked with designers to develop a program called zTemplates. I use it in every one of our listings and zTemplates is available to everyone. zTemplates can be found at ztemplates.com. Using your information, it creates a professional, high-tech, custom template for you that is different from anything anyone else has. It is very easy to use. You choose from over a hundred designs. If you're selling widgets and there isn't a template for widgets in the system, one is created for you. You enter your item description and policies, upload five photographs from your hard drive, and press a button. Instantly you receive the HTML to put into your listing. eBay does not charge you for this, because they don't do any of the work, and you save money on multiple-image hosting fees, because eBay is no longer hosting your photographs. Over time, this means a better bottom line for you.

zTemplates is extremely useful for branding, as it gives you a unique seller look. Moreover, it supplies you with a custom logo to put into every one of your listings. Buyers will be able to recognize you immediately just from the look of the auction. As compared to a standard eBay listing, when a buyer clicks on a zTemplate listing, they are more likely to stick around and check it out. The more they read, the more time they spend on your description, the more chance there is they're going to decide to bid.

Basic Listing

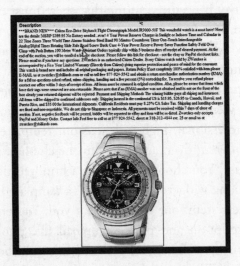

In a blind study, I asked a group of people which auction they would bid on. Both listings were for the exact same items, with the same payment and shipping policies. The overwhelming majority chose the professional template as opposed to the standard eBay listing. This study shows that if you're serious about your business, it clearly pays to look professional.

eBay recently sent out a report called "Best Practices." These are examples eBay has chosen as role models for the entire community. For the look of a listing, ours was recommended as best practices for a listing template. Certainly I was excited to be singled out, but more important, it told me that the work I was doing with

Template Listing

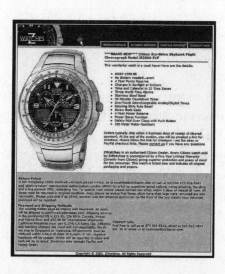

zTemplates is effective and makes an impact. Some people have asked why they should spend money on the look of their listing before they even know if their product is going to sell. This goes back to thinking like an entrepreneur. To find out if a product is going to sell, you have to give it the best possible shot at succeeding. When you consider the limitless potential eBay has to offer and the importance of the look of your listing and the perception that creates, the value of this investment becomes clear. If you were opening a physical store, it could cost you tens of thousands of dollars to find out if your product will sell. On eBay, a high-quality, professional virtual storefront will cost you a fraction of what the sign outside your retail store would cost. Compared to what I spent, a program like zTemplates is a minor investment. Compared to opening a brick-and-mortar retail store, the cost is downright tiny. As a matter of fact, just for reading this book, you are entitled to one month free of zTemplates. You can learn about this offer at the back of the book. Did you expect to be making money before you ever started?

About six months ago, a young woman came to one of my seminars in New York City. She had a great story. She was a former Miss Poland, who came to this country on her own when she was still rather young. A successful modeling career followed, and she retired two years ago. Unsure of what to do next, she bounced around a bit, searching for a new profession. In the midst of her search, a friend of hers told her about this new habit she had recently formed: eBay. This friend had signed on to sell a few things and now could barely put down her mouse.

They started selling together, and soon both of them were hopelessly hooked. The young woman still had all of her contacts in the world of high fashion and came up with a winning idea. She would use her network to gather clients dripping in couture and sell what they no longer wanted on consignment. Since she didn't invest in inventory but merely took a percentage of what she sold, she had almost no risk. By the time she arrived at my seminar, she was doing OK but wanted to take her business up a notch or two.

I decided to conduct a case study. On the left is the young woman's listing before she came to us. It was basic, dense, and uninteresting. Using zTemplates, she was given a custom design. She was clear as to what she wanted. Whereas I was eager to create the perception of a large corporation, she wanted the exact opposite. Pool tables are different from shoes. With fashion on consignment, buyers are looking for the great bargain. If they think they're dealing with a large company, they'll worry about built-in overhead and wonder if they can't find a better price buying from an individual. On the right is her listing using zTemplates. It is simple and sleek, sophisticated but not corporate. Even with her own listing, she was successful on eBay. Her feedback rating was already over three hundred. In our thirty-day test period, she had a 52 percent increase in conversions. Because she sells for clients, she cannot risk starting her auctions at $0.99, so she doesn't get much in the way of bidding wars. Her items either sell or they don't. She had a 52 percent increase in number of items sold and a 48 percent increase in the final price of those items. An item that had sold for $100 the month before now sold for $148. When I asked her if zTemplates was worth the monthly fee, she responded that it paid for itself on the first day of the month, and after that it went into business for her.

Let us return to the Canon Digital Rebel you've been selling. At the moment I type these words, there are seventy-four Digital Rebels for sale on eBay. If you follow the strategies outlined in this chapter, your listing will stand out. Your title will enable buyers to find you and will be specific enough that they will have only a handful of auctions to choose from. Because you have made use of the gallery and bold options, they will feel compelled to at least look at your listing. As soon as they click, they

Before   **After**

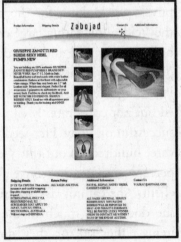

will encounter an attractive, professional layout with great images. Your description will be vividly accurate and answer any questions they can possibly think of. This will all serve to give prospective bidders the impression that you are a competent businessperson who cares about both the customer and the product you are selling. I can't guarantee that they're going to bid, but by this time, you've done everything you can to separate your listing from the eBay bunch. Thinking like entrepreneurs, we want a consistent, reliable result from the listings we post. In order to remain profitable, to manage our overhead and our cash flow as our business grows, we need something we know we can count on, something predictable. This system can provide that for us.

The Look of Your Listing

- Always use the gallery—it's the best $0.25 you'll spend on eBay
- Use boldface most of the time
- Try eBay's listing designer
- If you are so inclined, learn HTML
- Consider using third party site, like zTemplates, to host your listing

CHAPTER SEVEN

Photographs

A number of years ago, my cousin Steve got a call from a friend of his. His friend wanted Steve to go on a double date with him. Like many of us, he can't stand blind dates, but with his friend downright begging, he felt obligated to consider it. His friend swore he would like his date, whom he repeatedly referred to as "really cute." When Steve reluctantly told his friend that he'd think about it, his friend suddenly remembered he had a photo of her from a birthday party. He asked Steve to make a deal with him. All he had to do was look at the picture. If Steve did not like what he saw, he would leave him alone and forget the matter. Steve agreed and had to concede, when he viewed the photo, that there was some truth to the "really cute" comment. Steve went on the date. When he got to the Putt-Putt miniature-golf park at the prearranged time, the live version bore almost no resemblance to the picture he'd seen. Steve felt as if he'd been had. He still managed to win at miniature golf and have a good time on the date besides, but that is not the reason I tell this story. My point is that my cousin never trusted his friend after that. He was going to need more than a photograph if his friend wanted something out of him. It's an important lesson. If you want to be successful on eBay, your photographs better be more accurate than the one my cousin Steve was sold on, because the whole Web site is like one big blind date and people want what they pay for.

Buying online is a rather different experience from buying in a store. You can't pick up the merchandise, you can't feel it, smell it, taste it, or try it. The only sense a buyer gets to use is their sight. So the picture becomes paramount in their decision-making process. The quality of your photos will be a key determinant in the success of your eBay business. They must stand out.

If you're selling anything other than an original piece of art, or perhaps a rare collectible, you will have possibly hundreds of competitors out there, all peddling the exact same item. Aside from your shipping policy or your feedback rating, the only thing distinguishing you from all of those competitors are your photographs. When you look at it that way, you begin to realize that the images you capture are your single most important selling tool and perhaps the most important element overall in your eBay business. Even if you have a unique item, your images still have to sell it. In fact, if it's truly one of a kind, the photo becomes incredibly critical, because someone looking at it may never have seen anything like it before. If you've spent six months of your life creating and perfecting an abstract sculpture made entirely out of old Slinkys, and you want someone to buy it and put it on a pedestal in their living room, your picture has to be a compelling and accurate representation of it.

Your Photos Are Better Than Theirs

When I first started out on eBay, selling my first few pool tables, I spent a lot of time checking out my competition. I wanted to see how they ran their auctions, what kinds of policies they had, and how much their items sold for. I wanted to see who was successful and how they were achieving their success. I didn't know much about photographs beyond aiming my point-and-shoot at my daughter when she did something cute, which, of course, was all the time, but it still didn't teach me much about taking great photos. I began looking carefully at my competitors' auctions to see what their pictures looked like.

I wanted to know if I could learn anything from the images they were using. I did—I learned what not to do.

Most of the pictures of pool tables I saw on eBay were either unclear, uninteresting, or both. I don't know if these sellers didn't know how to take good pictures or if they simply didn't want to put in the time and effort required to create high-quality images. What I did know was I didn't want my photos to look anything like theirs.

I decided right then and there that any picture I ever used in a listing would jump off the page.

Your photos should bring your items to vivid life in a two-dimensional medium. If you can do that, people will F5 themselves to death for the honor of buying your product. From early on, I have been committed to the use of excellent imagery, and it has paid off big-time.

Let's say that you're selling an iPod mini. It's pink, it's brand-new in the box, and there are fifty-five others just like it on eBay right this very minute. An easy thing for you to do would be to go to Apple's Web site. They have a beautiful, professionally taken, perfect photograph of your portable little jukebox right there. You could take that and deposit it directly into your eBay auction. It's completely legal, as the manufacturer's pictures are in the public domain. These, however, are the only pictures you can take from someone else. If you notice that one of your competitors has a photo of the same pink iPod mini resting squarely on a black shag carpet and you think it's just a darling look.

Fun Fact

eBay policy forbids you from dragging that picture from your competitor's auction to use in your own.

If reported, your auctions will be shut down, and if you are caught repeatedly, eBay will ban you from the site forever. On the other hand, if you catch someone using your pictures, report them to eBay immediately. In a community policed by its members, this is not only your right, it's your responsibility. Be a Good Samaritan and help eBay maintain its honesty and integrity.

Before you use the legal and available public-domain photo, however, take a look at some of those fifty-five other auctions. You might notice that many of them have the same photo from Apple's Web site. If you take your own picture, you will immediately set yourself apart just by using something else. The difference alone will be enough to create interest in your auction and get people to look at your listing as opposed to everyone else's. It will also lend a sense of authenticity, as the buyer knows your picture shows the exact item they will be purchasing, as opposed to merely an example.

Strive for Photographic Genius

When using your own photo, it's a good idea to make that photo stand out. This doesn't mean you need to hire a model in a bathing suit to pose with the iPod. Rather, making a photo stand out on eBay can be as simple as having a good-quality, crystal clear image of your item. It can't hurt to try your hardest to make the picture you take of your item as close as possible to the best picture of that item on all of eBay. The pictures you take can show angles that other auctions' pictures don't show. It can give the potential bidder a more comprehensive feel for what they might be purchasing, filling in the sensory gap inherent in the world of Internet shopping.

Words of Wisdom

"There is real magic in enthusiasm. It spells the difference between mediocrity and accomplishment."   —*Unknown*

In the time a buyer spends conducting their search for a product, they will give your photo maybe ten seconds of their attention. In those ten seconds, you have to win them over. You have to convince them to choose you out of the crowd.

Quick Tip

A good photo can compel them to action.

It can make them think that if they fail to bid on your auction, they will miss out on the greatest pink iPod in existence.

They say a picture is worth a thousand words. In your picture, make five hundred of those words "buy" and the other five hundred "me."

Five Is Better Than One

Multiple photos of the item are highly recommended.

Fun Fact

> Statistically, it's been shown that if you have five photos of your item, you will sell much more of that item at higher prices than if have just one picture.

The first picture is free. After that it's $0.15 a picture. So, if you want five pictures in your listing, you're paying eBay $0.60 per listing on top of your listing fees—just for pictures, because they host the images. And if you know anything about the Internet, hosting images is not that expensive, except when there's traffic. And on eBay, with 115 million members, guess what? There's a lot of traffic. There are cheaper ways to host multiple images by forgoing eBay's hosting altogether and selecting one of the many hosting services out there on the Internet. More on that shortly.

What You Need to Start Taking Pictures: The Nuts and Bolts

Obviously, the first thing you need before you can become the Annie Leibowitz of the iPod world is a camera. If you already have a digital camera, great. If not, I recommend that you buy one. You can use your soon-to-be-dinosaur of a film camera, but I don't advise it. You will constantly have to buy film, pay to get the pictures developed and put on CD-ROM, or develop them yourself and then scan them into your computer.

> ### Quick Tip
>
> You will save yourself an extraordinary amount of time and money by purchasing a halfway decent digital camera.

It is one of the basic tools of the eBay trade.

Your digital camera is an incredibly valuable investment. You're launching a business with low start-up costs. One of the few things you need to worry about spending money on is a camera that can produce those amazing photographs just waiting to be taken. You don't have to spend a fortune to get a high-quality camera.

I strongly recommend that you purchase a three-megapixel camera or higher.

A couple of years ago, if someone had asked me what a megapixel was, the best I could have mustered in response would have been a blank stare. I'm still not a technical expert on digital photography, but I do know that a megapixel determines the size of the image you take. The more megapixels you have, the bigger your picture. Since you don't need a gigantic photograph, the picture gets shrunk down, and all those megapixels increase the quality of the image. From what I understand, megapixels are good things, and at any less than three you risk grainy, low-quality photographs. At the time of printing, a decent three-megapixel camera will cost you somewhere between $300 and $500. That's pennies on the dollar for the value you're going to get out of it. And you can save yourself even more money by purchasing it on eBay at a greatly reduced price.

There are a few features it would be beneficial to have on your brand-spanking-new three-megapixel digital wonder. You should be able to manually control the aperture, or f-stop. You also want a camera that can reach an f-stop of at least f16. Depth of field is the portion of your image that is in focus. The higher your f-stop, the greater your depth of field. There is no reason to get artsy with focus when it comes to product photography. Don't take a neat picture where only the screen of your iPod is in focus just because you can. No one wants to buy an iPod with just a screen.

Always use the highest f-stop possible, because that is how you will capture the biggest amount of visual information.

It would also be helpful to be able to control the shutter speed and the ISO rating. This is equivalent to film speed in the old cameras we're all used to. At the store, you'd pick up your 100 ISO film for outdoors, 200 ISO for indoors, 300 ISO for low light, and so on. With digital cameras, there is no film to buy, so the speed is controlled directly in the camera.

Another important feature to have is macro, which allows you to get very close to your subject without losing focus.

With macro, you can take clear pictures of very small details in your item.

Tush tags on Beanie Babies, serial numbers on electronic equipment, tiny scratches on an otherwise mint E.T. The Extra Terrestrial lunchbox— all of these can be shown large and clear with the use of macro photography.

Features to Look For in Your Camera:

- three-megapixel camera
- manual control of f-stop or aperture
- f-stop of at least f16
- ISO or shutter speed control
- macro

Setting Up Your Very Own Home Photo Studio

Now that your camera has arrived from the lovely seller on eBay, who was even kind enough to throw in a free carrying case, you have to set up a studio. Don't worry. Your wife's not going to kill you. You don't have to build Columbia Pictures in your dining room. All you need is a wall and a card table. Unless you plan on selling pool tables. Then you need a little more space. Let's assume you're not. No matter the size of your item, what you need is a white seamless background—unless your item is white. Then, I recommend you use something darker.

When I tell people to use a white background, some ask why they can't use yellow or blue or some other solid color. They can, but I don't advise it for two reasons. The first is that most pictures look better with a white background. It allows the item to take center stage. If that isn't reason enough, the second is that eBay listings themselves have white backgrounds. So the white in your photo dissolves into the white of eBay and it will all look like part of your listing. It's a very professional-looking touch.

Creating your sea of white is a very simple thing. Take the card table I mentioned earlier and put it up against that wall. Then get a large piece of white paper—it can be anything sturdy and smooth, like poster board. Tape one end to the wall and one end to the edge of the card table farthest from the wall. Curve it where the two meet, and no one will ever see anything but white.

If you have trouble creating that curve, use two separate pieces of paper. The difference will be minimal. You can also use a photo cube, which is a little plastic tent to house your item as you photograph it. Because it is plastic, your photo will often show a nice reflection right under your item when you use a cube. You can buy one in your local photo supply store or, as always, you can find one on eBay.

Another important element in your studio is a way to light your subject.

The entire purpose of setting up a studio, aside from avoiding the green shag carpet background so prevalent on eBay, is to avoid glare, reflections, shadows, and anything else that negatively affects the quality of your image.

Never ever use a flash.

The flash on your camera causes all these things and more, and when you are a product photographer, it is your enemy. Before you get nervous, you do not have to be award-winning cinematographer Lisa Rinzler to properly light your subject. All you need are two lights— any two lights you can direct at your item. Two table lamps will do. When you use only one light, you get a flat image. To accurately portray three dimensions of your item, use two. Put the stronger of the two to the side of your item. This is called the key light. The second you put next to the camera, to fill in the shadows created by the key light. Not surprisingly, this is called the fill light.

You can also use a window to light your subject. Daylight does not cause the same shadows as a single directional bulb. If you're using that photo cube I mentioned earlier, you need only one light source, because, as a translucent box, it automatically diffuses any light that enters it. On an artistic note, soft light works for any product you want to sell. If you have something shiny and of high value, however, like a piece of jewelry, you might want to consider more dramatic lighting, because it shows off sparkle a little more impressively.

Finally, get a tripod.

The higher your f-stop is, the lower your shutter speed will be. At low shutter speeds, your camera is susceptible to camera shake, reacting to even the tiniest vibration in your hand. But no matter how sensitive your camera is, it can't sense the vibration of a tripod. On eBay, you can find a pretty decent tripod for $10 or $15, a minor investment that goes a long way.

Elements of Your eBay Photo Studio

- Any wall
- Card table
- White poster board
- Two household lamps
- Tripod
- Photo cube (optional)

Your Images Tell the Whole Story: The Good, the Bad, and the Ugly

Use your images to tell a visual story. If you look at a Las Vegas Tables listing, my photographs constitute a virtual showroom. Do the same for your product. Feature small details. If there is a tag or a model number, show that. Be sure to include anything that distinguishes your item from others like it. The buyer may not be able to touch it, but after they see your pictures, they won't feel like they have to.

Take pictures of your item from multiple angles. With most products, it is good to have four or five different pictures in your listing. Show it off, but show its flaws as well. Make sure any dents, scratches, holes, discolorations, or anything else of the sort are clearly visible in your photographs.

I sold an old pair of sneakers on eBay recently. They were beat-up, stained, four-year-old sneakers. So I took pictures of the stains. I took pictures of the bottom of one to show that the tread was almost completely gone. I couldn't take pictures of the smell, but you could sense there might be one just from the visual information presented. These shoes were in bad shape. But I made sure to take pictures of everything that was bad about them. I didn't want someone to get them and say, "They polished them, they made them look presentable, but they didn't show the lousy tread or the side with the stains on it. They didn't tell me any of this before I ended up with this ratty pair of shoes." Even with every horrid detail featured in shining Technicolor, the sneakers ended up selling for $26.

Make sure all your images are in focus and well exposed. This in and of itself will put you three steps above half the people currently pushing their wares on eBay.

Take pictures in which your item fills the screen. An online marketplace is not the arena for wide shots. Use close-ups and keep your item centered in the frame. Make sure the color is accurately represented. There are many items—such as clothing, art, makeup, and so on—for which color is a crucial element. If, for some reason, the color in the photo is different from the item, say so in a caption. I sold a table recently. It was clearly stated in our listing that "Finished Color May Vary With Your Monitor Tags." Still, the customer who bought the table called me up and said, "This table is not cherry, it's mahogany. It's different from how it looked in your picture." I pointed out the statement in our policy, and, because of that, I was covered. If your picture doesn't represent your item precisely, say so. Sometimes you may need to use the words "Not Actual Size." This comes in handy for items like jewelry, where someone could misconstrue the size of the picture for the size of the item. I would definitely use this label with the diamond picture on page 213. If someone wants to buy a diamond ring and they don't know how big an eighth of a karat is, they might see this picture and expect something really big. They'll feel like they were misled.

Use "Not Actual Size" for anything that could be confused in this manner.

Those three words might be less important for, say, pool tables.

You can also place another object next to the one

you're selling, to show relative size. This works well with items that could be almost any size, such as a model airplane. If you do this, make sure the object you use is itself identifiable for its size. Also make sure it's different enough from your item so they don't wonder which one you're selling. The best thing to use in this case would probably be a ruler or measuring tape.

To avoid any potential misrepresentation, include dimensions in your listing so that there is no question of size on the part of the bidder.

From Your Camera to Your Listing: Editing and Uploading Your Photos

Taking your pictures is only half the battle. Now you have to get them from your camera into your computer, and then you have to edit them. It is very simple to transfer your images from camera to computer, and there are two ways of doing so.

Most cameras come with a USB cord, so you can transfer photos directly from camera to computer.

For Mac OSX users, the iPhoto program will automatically open up when it detects that a camera is connected. Otherwise, any photo software you use, whether it came with your camera or is independent of it, should have easy instructions to import your photos from the camera once it is connected. You can also use a memory card, for which you need a card reader. When you take a number of pictures and store them on multiple memory cards, the latter format is desirable. Unfortunately, there is no industry standard for memory cards, and different manufacturers use different ones, but they all do pretty much the same thing for you. Be aware of this, so that when you purchase your camera, your memory cards and your card reader are all compatible.

Once your photographs are safely ensconced on your hard drive, it's time to edit them a little. To do this, you need some sort of image-editing software. There are a variety of options out there, ranging from free to rather expensive. Among them, I recommend Adobe Photoshop Elements. It is easy to use, has a number of great features, and is relatively inexpensive. They even offer you a thirty-day trial period so you can see if it will really work for your needs. Photoshop is the full-blown, bells-and-whistles, industry standard for professionals. Elements is its consumer-priced version. Unless you are a serious photographer and image-editor, Elements has everything you will need for your eBay objectives.

Using Elements, Photoshop, or whatever other software you have decided to go with, edit out any minor imperfections in your photographic image—keeping in mind that you are not correcting for flaws in your actual item. I'm not suggesting you edit out stains or similar details on your item, as you want to be sure to include these as accurately as possible. You simply want to present your photographs in the best way possible. If your image is a little too dark, lighten it some. If the color is slightly inaccurate, you can correct that, too. You've seen all those models on the magazine covers. Nature didn't make them perfect, Photoshop did. You can do the same for your photos.

You will often find it useful to crop the background out of your image so that your item maintains its position center-stage.

This works remarkably well with the white eBay background we were discussing earlier.

There is one more feature Photoshop offers that I recommend you take advantage of.

Quick Tip

To protect your pictures from being stolen by other sellers, you can create a personalized watermark.

Use your logo, or User ID if you don't have a logo yet, and place it directly over your picture. No one will want to steal it, because it has your name on it. This is just like the "Kodak" you see on the back of your pictures when you get them developed. Turn the photo over, and there's no question as to who was responsible for the paper they're printed on.

Look at the figures on the next page. We took this picture against a white background but without using lights. When lights are used on diamonds, they reflect improp-

erly, so we had to do without. All we did in Photoshop was knock out the background. That's the only difference between the two pictures. It is amazing how smoothing out a few flaws and cropping some edges can improve the quality of your images. A good picture is suddenly an excellent one. Statistical analyses have shown that auctions using edited images actually sell more often and yield higher dollar amounts than auctions using the exact same photos in their unedited form. Spending just a little time at your keyboard can add dramatically to the bottom line of your business.

You now have fabulous pictures no sane buyer looking for your item could ever turn down. You still have to get them from your hard drive to your listing on eBay. There are a few ways of going about this. eBay itself allows you to upload one picture for free and additional ones for a nominal charge. If you use their service, the process is very simple. All you do is direct them to where on your computer the photos are stored and they do the rest for you.

You can also use a third-party provider to host your images. For a monthly hosting fee, you can upload any number of photos and images, and your hosting service will provide you a link that you can then direct your eBay listing to. eBay does not charge you at all for your photos if you use a third-party hosting service, no matter how many pictures you include in your listing. If you're an advanced computer user or have a current business that uses its own Web server, then you don't need me to tell you that you already have the means and equipment to bypass a third-party hosting service. For the majority of new eBay businesses, however, this will not be the case.

Using a third-party hosting service will eventually save you money if you are including multiple images in your listing, which you should be doing.

As I discussed in chapter 6, you can create your own personalized listings with a number of packaged third-party services available to you through the eBay network.

Your photos will be included in the personalized listings you create, so these full-package services provide an added layer of value to you, over a simple Web hosting service like High Five Domains.

For instance, zTemplates caters specifically to the eBay seller, so it lays out your listing description and photos in an easy-to-follow, step-by-step fashion, where the user-friendly quotient is high. You get image hosting and listing design all in one, in addition to a slew of added features to manage your selling on eBay. The final product is sleek, comprehensive, and looks like you spent a lot of money having it designed. It might not be long before the large hosting services like Yahoo! jump on the eBay seller–services bandwagon, so keep on the lookout for bigger and better deals on packaged hosting services.

In the end, just remember that your photographs will solidify your brand.

Quick Tip

The better your photos are, the more successful you'll be and the more you'll sell. If they are precise, sharp, and pretty to look at, you will increase both the number of bids you get on your items and the final price of your auctions.

Here is a handy, step-by-step summary to help you create and post fantastic photographs:

1. Get a digital camera with reasonable resolution, meaning at least three megapixels. This will allow you to produce high-quality images that you can easily edit.
2. Set up a small studio in your home or place of business. Create a nice, seamless, white background and light with a two-lamp system, window, or photo cube.
3. Take photos that include all the telling details.
4. Use image-editing software like Photoshop Elements to correct minor imperfections and crop out the background.
5. Upload the images to eBay or a Web-hosting provider.
6. If you use a third-party provider, place the URL or HTML code they supply you with into your auction listing to view the images.

Follow these steps, and your photographs will be among the best out there and you will profit from them.

Make it a rule never to list an item without exceptional photos. They are critical to the success of your business. There are hundreds of people selling the same items on eBay. Some are incredibly successful PowerSellers making hundreds of thousands of dollars a month. Some are mildly successful, and some aren't really successful at all. One of the main things separating them is the quality of their pictures.

Here's a key question to consider: If you were in the market to buy the item you're selling, would the picture you've taken be compelling enough to get you to buy?

The answer better be yes, because if you wouldn't be willing to buy it, why in the world would anyone else? If you would, then you're on your way.

CHAPTER EIGHT

Customer Service/
Feedback

I'm following the final moments of a heated watch
auction when the phone rings. Alice from customer
service asks me to take a complaint that's come in. I can
hear the anxiety in her voice. She's new. What she doesn't
know is that I get this call sometimes two, three times a
day. Something has gone awry and an incredibly irate
customer will speak to no one but me. I reluctantly pull
myself away from the action as she patches the call
through. Actually, I don't mind it. I like dealing with
people and I'm good at resolving their problems. In fact,
I bet I can slam-dunk this call in two minutes and still
be able to watch the last ninety seconds of the Citizen
Skyhawk barn burner. There isn't a problem associated
with pool tables I haven't seen before. Except this one. I
try to restrain myself from asking the buyer to repeat

himself, as I'm fairly certain I heard him right, but I can't resist.

"I'm sorry?"

"My crate's broken."

I did hear him right. A $2,500 pool table that he bought for a song in a no-reserve auction arrived in perfect condition five weeks ahead of schedule, and the guy is distraught that the shipping crate is a little banged up. I pull up our feedback page, and this gentleman has, indeed, left a scathing negative. Ignoring the Skyhawk entirely, I dig in.

Imagine that every retail establishment you patronize had to post the opinions of its customers right outside, in big, shiny letters. I do not think you would have to worry about rude salespeople ever again. Or at least not very often. On eBay, however, it's common practice. After every transaction, both buyer and seller have the opportunity to leave a positive, negative, or neutral comment for the other, based on the way they were treated during the process. These comments constitute your feedback rating. For every positive, you receive a point; for every negative, you lose a point; and there's no effect at all from a neutral. Your feedback page will show two different ratings—an overall number and the number of unique users. If the number of unique users is smaller than the overall number, you're getting repeat customers. That usually means you're doing something right. Not that a lack of it says you're doing something wrong, especially in the beginning, but repeat business is definitely a good sign. Your two ratings and the comments left for you are available by one easy mouse click to any prospective buyer or seller. They become your eBay reputation—your badge of honor or hall of shame, out in the open, for all to peruse at their leisure. As you build positive feedback, you attain different colored stars, marking your success as an honest and competent transactioneer. It's all about word of mouth, the eBay way.

Accountability Is King

Feedback is a basic eBay building block and one of the truly phenomenal things about it. It's the engine that drives the machine, keeping it square in the center of its lane. Like all things eBay, the feedback forum has simple but ingenious roots. The founders knew they could not involve themselves in individual disputes and maintain their core philosophy of offering a level playing field. Since they were not prepared to mediate themselves, they left it up to the community. It is one of the ideas that would make eBay the unique and remarkable entity it is today. Outside of 1600 Pennsylvania Avenue, there is no place in the world where you screw up and a hundred million people know about it. The level of accountability is unparalleled. eBay, as I have stressed, is a community made up of wonderful, genuine, and trusting people who hold you to what you say and let the world know if you don't live up to that.

Quick Tip

> Feedback is an invention that successfully calls people to act with integrity. In the world marketplace, that is revolutionary.

Feedback: Always on Your Mind

For your eBay venture to be profitable, you must think of feedback as real and crucial. It will absolutely affect the growth of your business.

There is a direct correlation between the percentage of positive feedback you have and the dollar value of your auctions. As the former rises, so does the latter. The likelihood of someone bidding on your items increases exponentially with the level of your feedback rating. If you are a buyer, the way to get good feedback is to pay and pay quickly. If you are a seller, there is only one surefire way to do so—provide stellar customer service. How many times have you been to a restaurant or store or other business that used to be fabulous and now isn't so much anymore? We usually call that "resting on one's laurels." On eBay, this is impossible.

Your most important feedback is your most recent, and the mechanism forces you to continue to provide good service over time.

Online or in the real world, customer service can make you or break you.

Customer service is also one of the things that allows you to compete with the big boys. Someone approached me the other day and said, "Best Buy just started selling on eBay. Best Buy! They're huge! Now no one's going to be able to sell electronics on eBay." Have you ever bought anything at Best Buy? Or even been inside? There is no reason to think their customer service online is going to be any better than what you can provide. Given the nature of any of the large-scale retailers and the proportional attention they can provide any one customer, I promise you, you're going to have no problem competing with Best Buy.

Excel in customer service and you will excel on eBay.

Providing good customer service on eBay is not rocket science. Above all else, you must constantly remember that the customer is incredibly important and that the service you provide them throughout the entire process will determine the success of your business. Everything grows from there.

This is where the concept of underpromise and over-deliver really comes into play.

You expect your buyers to pay you quickly, and they expect the same of you in regard to shipping. If you tell your customer you will ship within ten days and actually do so in three, they will be thrilled with the service you provide. Shipping fast, and faster than expected, is one of the key elements to building your necessary feedback.

You've Got Mail: Answer It!

There's an interesting quirk to eBay. The buyer's mentality on eBay is such that people think that you have only one item for sale and they are your only customer. They're the only one sitting in their den punching keys, so they must be the only one you need to deal with. It's not the same as when they have to take a number in a crowded deli. There they can see what you're up against. On eBay, the experience for the buyer is singular, even if you are dealing with as many people as Katz's. Because of this phenomenon, they expect an answer to their questions quickly, usually within an hour, and they expect your full attention. This may or may not be reasonable, but you still have to be aware of the expectation and do your best to meet it. Buyers often don't even identify themselves, or the item they're bidding on, in their communications to you. I can't tell you how many e-mails I've gotten where the entire e-mail would read something like, "What is the shipping cost?" or "Can you tell me about my order?" Obviously, the thing to do next is e-mail them back asking for their name and item number, but this fairly common behavior is indicative of how your customers feel.

If you get back to people quickly, you will make more
sales, because so many sellers do not respond quickly.

So many sellers take eons to get back to their customers and, unbelievably, some never do at all. Lightning-fast comprehensive responses will set you apart. Recently, I got an e-mail from someone at nine-thirty at night. I just happened to be online doing some work. The subject line of the e-mail said "second request." I looked and I thought, that's strange, because I check my e-mail all the time. And when I read the body of the note, it said, "I sent in a request for a question and I didn't get an answer yet, so I'm hoping you can get back to me as quickly as possible." I looked, and the first request was sent twenty minutes earlier. Now, it's not business hours, it's late at night, and still the twenty minutes it took me to get back to them was too long. I'm sure that this customer was simply excited about the item and wanted to bid but needed an answer before they felt comfortable doing so. Maybe they were in another time zone, or another part of the world, and they didn't even realize it was nine o'clock in Southern California. On eBay, this sort of thing happens all the time. It's part and parcel to managing a globe-spanning customer base.

Auction's Over, Time to Deliver!

Once the final seconds of the auction have ticked away and a bidder has risen above the fray to win your item, it's time to deliver the meat and potatoes of your five-star customer service. The first thing to do is contact your buyer immediately. They will recognize that this sale and they, as a customer, are important to you. Congratulate them on winning the auction, thank them, and outline again your payment terms and shipping policies. This letter will set the framework of what is to come, so the buyer knows exactly what to expect. They now have the option to pay based on your stated policies. With the ongoing integration of PayPal into eBay's seller services, you can have your customers receive an automatic preset e-mail from you, which you can personalize beforehand on PayPal. This allows them to pay immediately, often before you've even had a chance to view the closed auction.

Quick Tip

Once payment is received, ship the item as fast as possible and send a tracking number as soon as you have one. Speedy shipment generally equals positive feedback for you.

Every step of the way, from packaging to shipping to communicating the tracking number, your customer's future feedback comment should be on your mind. Often, the positive feedback comments you'll receive will mention your speedy shipping, just as the positive comments you'll leave buyers will often mention their speedy payment. As you know from the section on shipping and payments, there are a slew of options available for you to expedite your shipping process, and as the volume of your business grows, so do your options. Also, remember to protect your items in shipment, and to make sure that your packaging is, at the very least, *not* unseemly.

An attendee at a seminar I held recently in New York e-mailed me with a story about his trip to the post office to mail out his first batch of products to their respective buyers. When he got to the counter, the postal worker took one of his boxes and began adding her own layer of Priority Mail tape. The tape kept folding in on itself but she kept on going, leaving his box looking like it had been left to fend for itself in a day-care center stocked with Priority Mail tape and a dozen hyperactive toddlers. He was furious and asked that the box be replaced and resealed. "It's all about positive feedback, ma'am," he told her. This is not to say that you have to go to the same lengths for shipping aesthetics. However, what's important is that he had his feedback in mind. If you think something might affect your feedback negatively, then it might be worth your time to correct it before your customer receives their item.

If anything more than basic communication is required with a customer, sometimes it might help to get on the phone. A winning bidder's contact information will be available for you to access at a click. The more customer service you do on the phone, the more you'll sell. People like personal attention and they like knowing that they matter. A toll-free number is an easy, inexpensive thing to get, and you can include it right in your listings.

The Fundamentals of Great Customer Service

- Underpromise and overdeliver
- Answer questions in a timely manner
- Follow up and ship immediately
- Get on the phone when things get complicated

But this is only the beginning . . .

My mother is probably the greatest customer service rep ever. Her philosophy isn't unique, but she follows it with zeal. Ask her, and she'll tell you, "The way I want people to treat me is how I treat them." In other words, the Golden Rule.

Kindergarten stuff, you might think, but it works. You should see her in action. She gushes in her e-mails. There's actual gushing. She gives away more Beanie Babies than she sells, it seems. She loves throwing in an unexpected surprise and then seeing the reaction appear in the feedback or an e-mail. My mother has 100 percent positive feedback, which is not an easy feat. Six hundred fifty-eight feedbacks, all effusive. It shows in her sales, too. Even though Mom's prices are a little higher than her competitors', she sells those little stuffed beanbags in droves. Despite what you may think coming into the game, eBay is not simply about who has the lowest price. People want to have confidence in the people they're doing business with, and they want to be treated well. My mother takes this all very personally. If she got one negative feedback, she wouldn't sleep for three weeks. Her words, not mine. Learn from Mom. Customer service can be elevated to an art form.

Feedback Strategies

If you provide a quality service, and the transaction in question goes smoothly, 99.8 percent of the people are going to leave you positive feedback.

eBayers are conscientious and generally want to do the right thing by you. If they don't, feel free to ask them to do so. Let's say, a few days have passed since you've shipped your one-of-a-kind, signed Transformers: The Movie collectible, and you're certain they've received it, because you've checked the tracking number on ups.com. Still, every time you obsessively check to see if new feedback has arrived, your rating remains at the same number. At this point, you could send off a polite, friendly e-mail, saying something like, "I hope you have received your Optimus Prime limited-edition action figure. It has been a pleasure doing business with you. I would greatly appreciate it if you left positive feedback for me and I would be thrilled to do the same for you. Thank you so much for a smooth transaction." Feedback means a lot on eBay, especially when you are starting out and need to build your rating. If you have to resort to a little pleading, so be it. I did it, my mother did it, and, as she says, "Everybody has to start somewhere."

There are two schools of thought as to when you should leave feedback for the buyer. Many sellers leave feedback as soon as they are paid. I recommend that you wait to leave feedback until it is left for you. Feedback on eBay is transactional, meaning that only those directly involved in a sale can leave comments for each other, and they can do so only once, with a follow-up, if necessary. If you leave positive feedback for a buyer who has paid, and they then leave negative feedback for you, there is nothing you can do about the comment you have left. Unfortunately, eBay is host to a very small number of unscrupulous people who might use feedback as a form of what I like to call "legalized extortion." A customer will demand that you do something for them and threaten that if you don't, they will leave negative feedback. They might say, for example, "Your item arrived late. Even though your policy clearly states that you cannot guarantee shipping estimates, if you don't refund my shipping costs, I am going to leave negative feedback for you." You, as the seller, have two options. You can give in to their unreasonable demands, refund the money, and get positive feedback, or you can refuse them and risk getting negative feedback. If the buyer cares about their own feedback rating, they may not leave you the negative comment they have threatened, because you might do the same for them. If, however, you had left positive feedback for them as soon as you received payment, you have given up this powerful bargaining chip. Feedback on eBay is an emotional process. If someone gets a negative feedback, they will in all likelihood retaliate with one even if they were, up until then, happy with the transaction. Most eBayers are aware of this, too. As a seller, protect yourself. Withhold your feedback until the buyer has left you theirs.

Assume for now the buyer has left a glowing report for you on your feedback page, as will happen in a vast majority of the transactions, and you are ready to respond in kind. The next step is to figure out what you are going to do with your eighty characters of allotted space. Your comment should describe the transaction accurately. Feedback for a buyer is generally based upon the speed with which they pay. Typical comments include "fast payment," "smooth transaction," "great buyer!", "a pleasure to do business with," and so on, ad infinitum. There is no penalty for leaving these catchphrases for your customers. Some buyers might be more willing to buy from you again if you leave soaring compliments for them, and if the transaction truly transpired without a hitch, then there is nothing holding you back from boosting someone's feedback page. You'd want them to do the same for you.

You can also use your feedback comments as a selling tool. Take these eighty-character "real estate" opportunities to brand yourself. I write something like, "Great buyer. Fast payment. Thanks from LasVegasTables." This becomes one more place where you can leave an advertisement. On the off chance that someone out there looking at this buyer's feedback also happens to be looking for a pool table, they will see the name LasVegasTables and perhaps check us out. Think like an entrepreneur and brand yourself every chance you get.

Leaving Multiple Feedback

As your business grows, leaving individual feedback comments for each customer is going to become more and more of a time-consuming chore. eBay, thankfully, has made your job easier by allowing you to leave feedback for a group of transactions at once, instead of just individually. Many sellers do this once every few days or once a week, depending on their volume of business. This tool is a great time-saver and definitely something you'll want to take advantage of once you start selling in quantity.

Managing Negative Feedback

As you know from our previous PowerSeller discussion, it is important to note that in addition to grossing a certain number of dollars a month, you must maintain an excellent feedback rating to be a PowerSeller at any level. No matter how many sales you make, if your rating percentage dips below 98 percent, you can lose your PowerSeller designation. eBay is making a statement with this policy. How you treat people and how you conduct yourself as a transactioneer is of tantamount importance in this community. No honor will be bestowed upon you simply for moving a lot of product. You must behave according to the values outlined by the founders and upheld rigorously by the community at large. In other words, be a great seller, but also be a mensch.

As you approach PowerSeller status, or as you climb up the PowerSeller ranks, your system of feedback management will never lose its footing as a fundamental building block of your business. Rest assured that the more you have to deal with in terms of feedback management, the better you will get at managing it well. Good customer service will dramatically reduce your chances of getting negative feedback. Once you become a high-volume seller, however, it becomes virtually impossible to avoid negative feedback entirely. There will always be someone who is unhappy, and you should be prepared, because more than likely you are going to run into this.

If you are a large-volume seller, the issue becomes not so much whether you get negative feedback, but how you deal with it once it happens. You must manage the process diligently and intelligently.

In all of my eBay stores and auctions, I have a very firm feedback policy. Any customer who leaves negative feedback without first giving us a chance to resolve the problem will absolutely get negative feedback in return. I guarantee you, I will resolve any problem immediately, just give us a chance to help you. So if they give me a chance to help them, and then I don't, that's my fault. But if they just post a negative without giving me an opportunity to resolve the issue, they're getting one back. As I stated before, I don't leave feedback until it is left for me, and this is the reason why. I also state very clearly in my policy that anyone leaving positive feedback will receive that in kind, too, and I do so faithfully and in a timely manner.

Words of Wisdom

"Those who enter to buy, support me. Those who come to flatter, please me. Those who complain, teach me how I may please others so that more will come. Only those hurt me who are displeased but do not complain. They refuse me permission to correct my errors."
—*Marshall Field*

A nice thing about eBay is that very few people ever want to leave negative feedback. They will almost always contact you first if they are unhappy with some aspect of the transaction. They want to give you the benefit of the doubt and offer you a chance to make it right. Most of the time, when people leave negative feedback, they do so because they have had no response from the seller. Remember the guy who wouldn't let me pick up my item even though he didn't say "no pick-up" in the listing? I called him and tried my level best to resolve it. I told him that I wanted to work it out and had no desire to leave negative feedback for him. Without jumping the gun, I gave the seller every chance to make it right before I left my comment. Most buyers, you will find, are like that. Only rarely will you have to worry about negative feedback, but as I said before, it is going to happen eventually.

So you get a negative feedback. The first thing to do is not freak out. Try not to take it as personally as my mom would. It is not the end of the world, but do what you can to remove it. Sometimes negative feedback is deserved, sometimes it isn't, but deal with it and deal with it as quickly as you can. You have a ninety-day time frame for getting a feedback removed, but I wouldn't advise waiting that long. In my business, these things happen all the time. They keep coming, and I keep resolving them.

Oddly enough, the speed of our shipping has been at the heart of a number of our customer-service problems. I got one negative feedback just recently that read, "Will not return e-mails, bad customer service, won't reply to shipping status." I got on the phone to find out what exactly the problem was. It turns out this customer's table was shipped eight days after he paid for it, but he refused it when it arrived, because he switched the felt color after we had already sent it out. I had told him it would take six weeks to ship, but he changed his mind in two, so he said we shipped too fast. Once I let him talk and calmly explained our side, I was able to quickly resolve the issue.

eBay has policies. It is important you know and obey them, as I discovered the hard way early in my online career, but you can also learn how to make them work for you. I became a pro at this, especially in regard to managing feedback. There are ten reasons eBay will consider removing a negative feedback:

10 Reasons eBay Will Consider Removing Feedback

1. The feedback is left by a user who supplied fraudulent information when registering at eBay.
2. The feedback contains any personal identifying information about a user.
3. The feedback in question has no relation to eBay—such as comments about transactions outside of eBay or personal comments about users.
4. The feedback is comprised of profane or vulgar language.
5. The feedback is left by a user as part of harassment.
6. The feedback is left by a person who can be identified as a minor.

7. The feedback contains a link to another page, picture, or Java script.

8. The feedback is intended for another user, when eBay has been informed of the situation and the same feedback has been left for the appropriate user.

9. The feedback refers to any investigation whether by eBay or a law-enforcement organization.

10. eBay is served with a court order stating that the feedback in question is slanderous, libelous, defamatory, or otherwise illegal. eBay will also accept a settlement agreement from a resolved lawsuit submitted by both attorneys and signed by both parties, as well as ruling by a certified arbitrator where both parties agreed to submit the issue for binding arbitration.

Familiarize yourself with them. First on the list is that the person leaving the feedback has to have valid contact information on file with eBay. So the first thing I do when I get a negative feedback is download the customer's personal information. This option is available to both buyer and seller in a transaction. If you find the phone number or e-mail address is no longer current, the feedback is immediately eligible to be withdrawn by eBay upon your request. Therefore, calling them and praying that their phone is disconnected is a valid first approach. I still resolve all issues with the client, but this is one of the quickest ways to make negative feedback disappear forever.

I became so good at making eBay's feedback removal system work in my favor that I was unwittingly instrumental in their changing one of my very favorite policies. If someone puts your actual name instead of your User ID in a feedback, then that comment is automatically eligible for withdrawal. So if someone leaves me a negative feedback that says, "Adam didn't do what he said," it will automatically be removed, because the customer used my name. I got really, really good at getting negative feedback removed because it had my name in it.

When somebody leaves you feedback that is less than positive, you want to do two things. You want to resolve the complaint quickly with the customer, and you then want to ask them to post a follow-up. I would call the person, and I would say, "Thank you very much. I'm glad we got this resolved. Great. Now if you could do me a favor and update your feedback on eBay." They'd inevitably say OK, and I would always jump in with, "What I want you to do is put in the feedback, 'Follow-up: Spoke with Adam, issue resolved.' " Then, as soon as it posted, I'd fire off an e-mail to eBay, complaining that my name had been used in the feedback, and they'd remove it for me. Great system.

Then they changed the policy. They didn't tell me, either. I had about five people whom I had just done this with, so I sent the e-mail to eBay, and when I checked my feedback, it was all wrong. The original comments were still there, but the follow-ups were gone. The newly rewritten policy says that if your name is in the comment, it is still removed, but here's the trick. They no longer remove the entire comment but simply the part your name is in. So I lost all my great follow-ups, and now all I had left were these negative comments that couldn't be followed up again. They got me back. Don't mess with these eBay guys. They're serious.

Square Trade and Mutual Feedback Removal

So you go through the ten criteria, and the negative feedback mocking you from your computer screen is ironclad as far as eBay policies are concerned. There are still two avenues available to you to remove the feedback from your rating. The second has pretty much eliminated the need for the first, but I'll discuss them both.

Square Trade is an independently affiliated third-party mediation company and Web site. They bring two parties together to resolve disputes. Most people who use Square Trade—I would say, 99.9 percent—use it to do just that. Not me. I used it as a feedback withdrawal tool. Up until recently, filing and resolving a case with Square Trade was the only way to get legitimate feedback removed. Since I deal with all of my customer service problems internally, I don't need Square Trade to mediate for me. I do that myself, and you might consider doing the same. When I filed a case, the issue would already be resolved. I would simply go through the process with the buyer, who by this time was happy with me, in order to remove the feedback. It costs $20 to open a case with Square Trade. People would ask me why they should pay that much to deal with a dispute involving, say, a $10 item. I would remind them that their feedback rating is their entire reputation and word of mouth on eBay, and that is worth a lot more than $20.

On February 9, 2004, eBay implemented a new tool that all but eliminates at least my need for Square Trade. It's called Mutual Feedback Removal, and it's going to save you a ton of $20 bills. You can now be your own Square Trade. If you leave me negative feedback, my first step will still be to get on the phone and talk you through it until you are satisfied.

Now, instead of paying Square Trade to tell eBay to remove the feedback, we can do it ourselves through Mutual Feedback Removal. The comment will remain alongside a follow-up, but the negative mark goes away and no longer affects the overall rating.

Here's another example where the speed of our shipping landed us another negative feedback. A woman bought a watch. She realized afterward that she would need extra links, an option available in her auction for an additional fee. Instead of calling us, she ordered the links online and paid for them immediately. Well, once again, this item had already shipped. When it arrived a few days later, minus the extra links she paid for, she was upset and pulled the feedback trigger before even contacting us. I contacted her immediately, of course, and was able to resolve the issue quickly. What I didn't do, however, was say, "Thank you and please use Mutual Feedback Removal once you get off the phone." Instead,

I stayed on the phone and walked her through it, making sure that by the time I got off the phone, I could check my computer and the negative sign would be gone.

I always take the extra step and make sure the customer knows exactly what to do and how to do it. In fact, if they're open to it, try to keep them on the phone until the entire process is taken care of. Often, they are so happy their issue has been resolved they will even ask you what you want them to say. Personally, I love when that happens. Go ahead and take advantage of this opportunity to color your feedback page pretty. You certainly can't control your feedback any better than that.

Before you start shedding tears for Square Trade, don't worry. They're not going out of business any time soon. First, most people, as I stated earlier, use it to mediate because they aren't inclined to do so for themselves. Second, there are a few instances where even great mediators like you and I can use the help of a third party. There may or may not come an instance in which you'll deal with someone who is so set in their argument that you will be unable to find an acceptable resolution.

If you do reach such an impasse, the best thing to do is open a case with Square Trade.

Another smart time to do so is if you have a buyer who simply refuses to discuss the dispute with you.

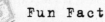

Fun Fact

On Square Trade, if the other person fails to respond within fourteen days, the feedback is automatically removed.

A lack of response from them might indicate that they do not want to deal with the issue any longer, or it might be that they went on vacation or deleted the e-mail accidentally. Either way, it's an easy fix for the problem and certainly worth the shot. Square Trade doesn't charge you unless mediation actually occurs, so in these cases you'd have the feedback removed for free.

You can also use Square Trade as a preemptive strike. If someone merely threatens to leave negative feedback, you can go ahead and open a case. Most of the time, I don't recommend this, as you should be able to talk to the person and work out whatever issue they have, but it comes in handy in cases involving that legalized extortion I mentioned earlier. If someone tells you they plan on leaving negative feedback unless you do something for them that is out of the realm of your agreement, Square Trade may be the way to go. For example, a guy bought a digital camera from me and then sent an e-mail with an outrageous demand. There was still plenty of time to ship the camera within the terms agreed upon, but he said if the item hadn't shipped already, he would either leave negative feedback or I could refund his money plus 50 percent. Instead of giving in to what essentially was blackmail, I opened a case with Square Trade, explaining to them what was being threatened.

If something like this happens to you and you're fairly certain you won't be able to get the person to see reason, use Square Trade as a way to prevent the negative feedback before it even happens.

As you see, there are a few ways to go about getting a negative or even neutral feedback removed. No matter which you use, I recommend you get on the phone and deal with the buyer directly. It's my opinion that you can't resolve feedback issues through e-mail. In addition to being less personal, it allows much more room for misinterpretation on the part of the reader. Talk to the people. Listen to their problems. Do less of the former than the latter. Whether they are right or wrong is irrelevant. Figure out the root of the problem, let them work through it themselves, and push them gently in the desired direction. You'll be amazed at how little you have to actually say to appease your customers. Don't get me wrong. You're still going to have to say things, and the right things at that, but listening is your key to success here.

What's Your Feedback Score, Chum?

I should note that as ingenious as I think it is, my mother hates the feedback system. Like I said, she takes it to heart, and she is such a good person that she doesn't see why people can't settle things without resorting to something like leaving negative feedback. Her worst nightmare is that some "schmuck" who had a fight with his wife is going to take it out on her in the form of negative feedback, ruining her well-deserved perfect score. I understand what she's saying, but it's hard to imagine eBay being as successful as it is without the kind of feedback system they have developed over the years, especially with the addition of Mutual Feedback Removal. You have recourse now.

Feedback is an extremely valuable tool. It is the eyes and ears of your customer service, telling you the quality of both your product and how you run your business. Think about how many companies and establishments beg and bribe you as the consumer to tell them how they are doing. At restaurants, they sometimes give you a form to fill out with your bill; at hotels, the form is frequently on your pillow the last night of your stay. On eBay, people voluntarily provide you with this kind of information on a consistent basis. You know almost immediately what makes your customers happy, what upsets them, and what brings them back for repeat business. You can actually monitor and have an effect on your own word of mouth. There's nothing like it anywhere else in the world—or in life, for that matter—and with all due respect to Mom, I expect the feedback system to continue being the glue that keeps eBay's business together.

eBay's feedback system has even affected the way business is run in the offline world. It has been a powerful force for reform. Until eBay launched eBay Motors, one of the most miserable tasks for the American consumer was buying a used car. Stan in the loud checkered jacket always seemed to be talking out of both sides of his mouth. Stan was a very difficult character to trust. Well, now, if Stan wants to increase his sales with a presence on eBay, he has to compete with individuals merely trying to get the best price they can for their old Honda Civic. They have no reason to put on the song and dance Stan has spent years perfecting. And even if Stan doesn't want to sell on eBay, he knows that if his real live customers are unhappy with his service, they can always go home, get on the computer, and leave him in the dust.

The power dynamic has changed, and Stans across the country have been cleaning up their act, and the used-car-buying experience has improved immeasurably. This holds true for a number of industries, and the level of customer service you've learned to expect on eBay will begin to seep into every consumer market we have. I'll share with you here a compelling, if amusing, prediction from an economist friend of mine on the future relevance of eBay's feedback system:

> I see a future in which every man, woman, and child who can use a mouse is on eBay. You carry an eBay debit/credit/ID card. With one swipe, anyone you come into contact with can see your feedback rating. The credit history companies go out of business, because people no longer use them as an indicator. Anyone you have any sort of interaction with anywhere can give you feedback. eBay is only one area where people can rate you. Sections include family, friends, employment—if you treat a waitress poorly, she can put that in your per-

manent feedback score. When someone says, "This will go down on your permanent record," it is no longer a joke. Square Trade becomes a trillion-dollar business—opening up physical courts to solve disputes. Court TV opens a sister channel focused only on feedback cases. It becomes the most successful cable channel in history. When you go to a job interview, feedback is the only thing they want to look at. Sexual partners chime in with their two cents in the Mature Audience section. eBay is the new Big Brother.

I guess it's a good thing you care so much about your feedback.

So here I am, sitting on the phone, trying to work things out with the crate guy. Here's what I don't understand. The crate that the pool table is shipped in has one and only one purpose. It protects the pool table. The key is for the pool table to arrive at your home undamaged, so we put it in a crate. What was he going to do with the crate after it arrived? He didn't buy the crate for the crate itself. He bought it for the pool table. The pool table was perfect, but he wanted $100 back for the crate, because it was broken. I could not, for the life of me, figure out what he was going to do with this thing. Did he want to resell it? Turn it into a playhouse for his kids? As I'm talking him through it, I begin to understand. He paid for a crate, so he thought he should get one in decent shape. I explain all about the crate's reason for being and how the damage it has suffered is proof of its necessity. I make sense, and he realizes that. Together we go through the mutual feedback removal process, and everyone is happy. I look back at the computer. The bidding on the Skyhawk is over. It sold for 30 percent more than usual. All in all, it's been a good night.

Customer Service

- Provide stellar customer service
- Underpromise and overdeliver
- Respond to e-mails as quickly as possible
- Contact buyers as soon as the auction is over
- Ship quickly and send tracking numbers
- Pack it up pretty
- Get on the phone

Managing Feedback

- It is OK to request positive feedback for a smooth transaction
- Leave feedback *after* it is left for you
- Use feedback as another opportunity to brand yourself
- As your business grows, leave feedback in batches

If You Get a Negative Feedback

- Check contact information and eBay's other criteria for eliminating feedback
- Resolve problems on the phone and use Mutual Feedback Removal to eliminate the negative
- Walk them through the process to make sure it is completed correctly
- Use Square Trade as a last resort, and preemptive strike if necessary

Part
Four

Taking It to
the Next Level

CHAPTER NINE

Growing Your Business

When I started selling pool tables on eBay, my commute consisted of walking downstairs from my bedroom to the basement. A short hallway and eighteen steps were all that separated my bed from my place of business. If I wanted to listen to Howard Stern during my trip, I had to walk very, very slowly. I started to really resent having to go to work, because not only was the eBay commute unbeatable, but I was making more money from home than I was at the store.

My eBay office was in my home right from the very beginning, and I initially intended to keep it there. I live in a town house in Los Angeles with my wife, Jennifer, and my daughter, Haley. I had only one room in the house for me, and that room, my study, was in the basement. This is where I had my desk, and my computer, and the entirety of my eBay operation. I hired someone to work for me in November 2002 and put another desk in the corner. Then I hired someone else to work for me, so I got rid of my couch. When I hired a third person, I got rid of my big, swiveling, bells-and-whistles designer chair that I had acquired through a dot-com bust fire-sale, and replaced it with four small office chairs, one for each of us. Each person I hired had to build their own small desk their first day on the job. The desks were delivered by Staples, and day one on the job was desk assembly. I later found out eBay started this way, too. Everyone, no matter what their position at eBay, was given a kit and a screwdriver and required to build their desk in the early days of the company that makes my business possible. I had one desk in each corner of the room, and though we were cramped, it worked. That is, until my wife confronted me just two weeks into the operation.

"Three women in the house with you is enough." It was actually five women, if you counted Jennifer and Haley. "I don't want any more women in the house— time to go get an office."

That was it. No discussion. I'd been evicted from the basement. That's why I got an office. We hadn't necessarily outgrown our home-office space; we had just outgrown our landlord's patience.

Whether you work out of your home, as is the case for the majority of eBay sellers, or out of an office, as has become the case for some of us, you can benefit equally from running your own show. Setting up and managing

your own eBay business in a disciplined manner is essen-
tial to reaping those benefits.

About six months after I sold my first pool table, with my eBay income looking like it was ready to take over for me full-time, I figured it was time to have an experienced consultant come in and help me organize my business. I was referred to a financial planner who agreed to come by the office that week to assess my eBay business. The next day Will Rogers and I met in my office, and after chatting about eBay for several minutes, we got down to business.

"So, Adam, tell me about your record keeping."

I gave him a blank stare for a moment, then looked over his shoulder and pointed. "See those boxes in the corner?" There were two large boxes stacked knee-high with bills, files, paper receipts, and whatever else managed to end up in the corner that could have had a sign over it, reading, "Whatever It Is, Toss It Over Here."

"It's all right there, Will," I said.

Up to that point, I hadn't come to the realization that I was actually running a business. I knew that at the end of the month I had more money than I started the month with, and that was all I cared about. What's more, I was having fun, and it was exciting for me to be on eBay. Will has since become an eBay expert himself. He works with other sellers on eBay and advises them on setting up their own businesses. Will helped me realize that this was really a business and not just something I was doing for fun. For every eBay entrepreneur and aspiring PowerSeller, growing your business and reaping the benefits of a home-based operation requires setting up a sound foundation that can, to put it simply, make your business legit.

Words of Wisdom

"The total worldwide value of goods and services purchased by businesses through e-commerce solutions will increase from $282 billion in 2000 to $4.3 trillion by 2005."   —International (IDC)

There's an underlying motivation behind starting a home-based Internet business, no matter what the nature of the business. Small-business entrepreneurs are captivated by the idea of starting an income-generating machine with little overhead, and of being the boss of that operation. Small-business owners are also aware of the potential of lucrative rewards in the future from their venture. There are underlying challenges to this worthy goal, and those challenges are not so different from those faced by traditional brick-and-mortar businesses. The challenge of managing a growing business operation can be daunting, especially when someone is caught unprepared in the midst of rapid business growth. Taken step by step, however, the challenge of developing an effective business system becomes a very manageable one. The key is to prepare and execute your business systems in a disciplined manner, regardless of what point you find yourself on the business growth curve.

Record Keeping

Quick Tip

One of the most important things to do for the long-term success of your business is set up an accounting system.

In the beginning, I failed completely at the job of bookkeeping. My strengths were in sales. I was concerned with creating better auctions, providing great customer service, and increasing profits. My strengths were not the day-to-day management of the financial and accounting aspects of my business. I needed a way to manage my receipts, my expenses, my bill collection, my customer database, and so on. I had no idea how to do any of this.

One of the best things Will did for me was introduce me to Quickbooks Pro.

Of all the bookkeeping software, Quickbooks Pro is the easiest for the layman to learn and use. Most people don't get into business because they excel at accounting. I sure didn't. In fact, many of us are intimidated by the whole process, which is why I just threw everything into a box. Quickbooks allows me to manage all of the financial aspects of my business in a simple and efficient manner.

Track and Analyze

All businesses have to conduct some sort of bookkeeping. In a retail store, the cash register spits out a daily print-out. This immediately tells the owner or manager exactly how much money has been made that day, that week, that month, and that year. There is no cash register in an eBay business. People would ask me how my sales were, and I would invariably say, "Good." I wasn't trying to be coy. I knew that I had more money in my bank account than I did the week before, but I didn't have any clue as to how much. I was having a great time creating listings and watching the bidding, but I absolutely did not have my finger on the pulse of my business.

Quickbooks allows me to measure exactly that. It tells me precisely how profitable my business is or is not. The whole idea of creating an eBay business is to give us the financial freedom to realize our dreams. Often, someone quits their job to start a business and ends up only more of a slave to that business than they ever were to their previous employer. Understanding what makes your business profitable and what doesn't will help you avoid that trap. In addition, organizing your books properly in the beginning will save you an enormous amount of time, effort, and heartache in the long run. You won't have an overwhelming box of little notes and receipts that comes to life as a giant paper monster in your nightmares.

Tracking and analyzing their financials is incredibly empowering for small businesspeople—auto mechanics,

restaurateurs, contractors, and eBayers alike. Many
people fear numbers and accounting, but when they
learn the basics and see how the financial aspects
of their business give them new clarity, they come to
appreciate and perhaps even enjoy keeping their books.

When you have a true understanding of how inter-twined your accounting, management, and marketing are with your actual sales and bottom line, you begin to make informed decisions. You know if hiring an additional employee makes sense. You know whether you should invest in a new piece of equipment or when to start a new product line. You have hard data pointing you in the direction of good, sound decisions for your business. A good accounting system provides you with the knowledge of what will increase your profitability.

eBay, for example, offers a number of listing en-hancers at additional costs. For $0.25 you can post a gallery picture. For $1 you can display your title in bold lettering. For $19.95 you can have your item featured at the top of the category page. Without the ability to properly analyze your business, there is no way to know whether these investments are effective and whether they add or subtract from your bottom line. Now I use in-depth analysis of the numbers to determine the steps I should take at every stage of the game. Good record keeping and analysis is the only way I know that gallery is the best $0.25 you can spend on eBay, that bold makes sense most of the time, and that featuring an item is usually a waste of money.

You can use these analyses for every area of your eBay business—your listing format, your shipping methods, the amount of inventory you purchase, your pricing strategies, ad infinitum. Often people measure their businesses using the wrong benchmark. They look at the amount of traffic they create or the overall number of successful sales they make. The only true determinant for the success of your business is your profitability. If you use your bookkeeping to analyze and track your business, you will always know what is making you money and what isn't. Throughout this book, I have discussed experimenting with a variety of strategies and products. An experiment generally consists of stating a hypothesis, or a guess as to how the experiment will go, testing that hypothesis, and forming a conclusion based on the results of the testing. Without proper book-keeping, you won't know what conclusions to draw from your carefully tested experiments.

Get Some Advice

Fortunately for those of us who dread dealing with accounting, one intelligent option is hiring a bookkeep-er. They will run Quickbooks for you and provide you with all the information required to track your business. Finding a bookkeeper is a relatively simple process. Most accounting software companies maintain a referral database of professionals certified in that program. I gen-erally recommend Quickbooks, because not only is it user-friendly, but it is the accounting software of choice for most accountants and small businesses in this coun-try. You will have no trouble at all finding a bookkeeper who knows the program. I found Will by contacting

Quickbooks. They have a certified-advisor database and will give you a list of competent professionals in your area who can assist you.

Bookkeepers charge either an hourly rate or a monthly retainer fee, depending on the amount of work that needs to be done. For a small business, a bookkeeper will generally cost between $200 and $500 a month. This may seem expensive, but in the long run, a bookkeeper will pay for themselves many times over. The amount of money a bookkeeper saves in keeping the books and giving tax advice is significant. Still, a monthly service may be cost-prohibitive when you're just starting out, so you can initially hire a bookkeeper to teach you how to do your own books until your business grows enough for you to afford the expense of a retainer or hourly fee. In fact, doing your books yourself in the beginning will really help to educate you about your finances and the inner workings of your business.

There is a value in hiring professional advisors to guide you in your eBay venture. They are educated in the current financial environment and will assist you in making informed decisions for your business. They can help you figure out whether you should secure a loan and how to do so. They will advise you on raising capital and taking on partners. They will aid you in determining where to invest and where to cut costs. They can help you steer your business in the direction it needs to go.

In addition to a bookkeeper, I recommend hiring an attorney, at least to help in the forming of your corporation and also for some of the legal issues that generally arise in the early days of any financial venture. It is also a very good idea to involve a tax strategist at the very beginning. They will help you deduct as much as you possibly can as soon as you possibly can. Tax strategists pay for themselves many times over. I will discuss tax strategies and deductions in depth in the next chapter, but it is important to know there are a number of benefits you can take advantage of immediately after starting your business. This can increase the amount of money in your bank account before you even make your first sale.

When you are searching for advisors, I recommend going to dkacpa.com. Diane Kennedy is the author of *Tax Loopholes of the Rich* and I will discuss her further in the next chapter as well. This is her Web site, and you can download an "Advisor Checklist" there for free. It will provide you with a list of questions to ask any advisor you're considering hiring for your business. Questions like, "Where did you go to school?" and "How much do you charge?" are less important than questions about their point of view and experience. Find out what they specialize in and what kind of clients they have. You want someone who has clients with businesses just like yours. Diane's clients are exclusively those who have businesses or invest in real estate. Some firms specialize in specific types of businesses or sectors of the economy. Find a match that fits your venture.

If you are starting an eBay business, you want to hire people who have an understanding of the laws and benefits associated with Internet ventures.

There's no point in paying to train them. By asking questions, you can ensure that you are hiring people who will do exactly what you need them to. You do not need to find advisors in your local area. Advisors can be from anywhere. Diane has some clients she's never met face-to-face. Everything is done by phone, fax, and e-mail. With an Internet business, you're open for business everywhere. It doesn't matter where your advisors are, because the issues and points of law are generally the same for everyone. There are, however, special issues related to Internet businesses, so make sure they have experience in the virtual environment. You may want to hire a local bookkeeper for your day-to-day accounting and an Internet specialist to help with your tax strategies.

Automate

Once you are running one hundred auctions a month or more, I recommend exploring the option of auction management software. It will save you an incredible amount of time and effort, because it automates much of the auction process for you. When you list on eBay, you are constantly entering in data. Doing this manually, as we all do in the beginning, is time-consuming. Auction management software eliminates much of this work. As soon as an auction ends, it will send a winning-bidder notice to your customer, informing them of their total and your preferred payment methods. When payment is made, it will record that information and then create a UPS, FedEx, or U.S. Postal Service shipping label for the package. If an item doesn't sell, the software will relist it.

When you're doing all of this yourself, it is easy to get behind. Sales begin to build up, begging for your attention. If you get too far behind, you may start shipping late and customers will not be happy. You may start to feel incredibly overwhelmed. The first day you put your auction management software to work will be one of the happiest days of your eBay life.

The auction management software I recommend is called My Auction Generator and can be found at myauctiongenerator.com. It synchronizes with Quickbooks, which further reduces the amount of data entry necessary. The more integrated your systems are, the more automated your process will be.

Fun Fact

When Zoovy completes its post auction service, it then transfers the information from that auction to your Quickbooks database.

This is one more step you don't have to take anymore. If you're doing two hundred auctions a month, these programs will save you hours and hours of data entry.

Legitimize

Once you decide to make your eBay pastime a legitimate business, there are a few steps you have to take. They are the same steps you'd have to take if you were starting a traditional brick-and-mortar store. Many people think that Internet businesses follow an entirely different set of rules, since they operate in cyberspace instead of in a minimall, but that is actually untrue. In the eyes of the United States government, a business is a business.

Choose a Business Entity

The first thing you have to do is determine what form your business is going to take.

You may decide you want to be a sole proprietor, meaning that you are the one and only owner of your business. You may decide to operate with a group of people as a partnership, or form a corporation. Each one of these entities has different legal and tax ramifications. If you are sued by a customer or accrue debts the business can't repay, your personal assets have different legal protections depending on which form your business takes. This is a key decision, as it is the basis for your future operations.

Originally, I operated my business as a sole proprietor. I sell thousand-pound items that carry with them more legal issues and liabilities than most items. When I met Will, he advised me to form a corporation to increase my legal protection, limit my exposure, and increase my tax benefits.

To determine the right entity for your business, examine the size of your business and assets. My situation is different from the majority of eBay businesses. I have an inventory size exceeding $200,000, so I needed to form a corporation to separate my business assets from my own personal assets. If you are starting a small business and just building revenue, you may want to form a sole proprietorship. This is also called a Schedule C business, because it is reported on Schedule C of your tax form. It is the least costly method of forming a business and the easiest to set up. The problem with a sole proprietorship is that as you start making money, you're going to have to pay an extra self-employment tax of 15.3 percent on top of your regular income tax. The second problem with a sole proprietorship is the risk involved. If you get sued or the business goes into debt, all of your personal assets are at risk. I generally recommend moving out of a sole proprietorship as soon as your business begins generating a sizable profit.

If you are looking to start a business generating a higher volume and requiring a large investment, or your business has progressed beyond the early stages, you should look into forming a corporation. If you are selling vintage T-shirts and your initial investment is a few hundred or a few thousand dollars, consider a sole proprietorship. If, on the other hand, you plan on selling electronics and your initial investment will be $50,000 or $100,000, consider forming a corporation. No matter what you do, it is a good idea to involve a professional advisor to assist you in your decision-making process.

If you decide to go for a corporation, formats to look

at are Limited Liability Companies, Limited Part-
nerships, S-Corporations, and C-Corporations. Many
business consultants suggest the S-Corporation for people just starting out. You can do this at the state level,
over the Internet, on your state government's Web site,
although I do encourage you to solicit the aid of an attorney for the process. It will cost you a much greater
amount in the long run to fix any mistakes you make
than to hire assistance and do things properly in the first
place. Once you set up your corporation, you inform the
IRS that you wish to be taxed as an S-Corporation. You
will now take some of your income as salary, and the rest
in distributions. Distributions are not subject to any kind
of payroll tax. The usual progression for most eBay businesses is to begin operations as sole proprietorship and
eventually move to an S-Corporation.

Get a Tax ID Number

*After deciding on the proper entity for your business, the
next step is to acquire a tax ID number.*

This is a federal tax number you get directly from the
Internal Revenue Service. If you go to irs.gov, you can
download Form SS4 Application for an Employer
Identification Number. This will be the identifying
number of your business. You will use it to file both
income tax returns and payroll tax returns if you have
employees.

Open a Checking Account

If you choose to form a sole proprietorship, it is important to open a separate checking account just for your business.

I failed to do this in the early days of my pool-table selling hobby, and I had no sense of where money was coming from or going to. I wrote checks for the plumber and my wife's birthday gift from the same account I used to pay for my eBay fees. There are a few problems with this. The first is the confusion caused. You certainly can't have your finger on the pulse of your business if you don't know what's coming from where and what's going where.

The main reasons for segregating your personal and business accounts are for tax and credibility purposes. The IRS requires precise, clean record keeping. A dedicated bank account is the only way to do this. In addition, you may be required to provide financial statements to lending institutions, possible investors, and vendors. Comingling your personal and business finances can damage your credibility and the perceived strength of your business.

Fictitious Names

If you give your business a name other than your own, you are required to file a fictitious business name in order to open a checking account and conduct your affairs.

LasVegasTables needs a fictitious business name, but Adam Ginsberg Pool Tables does not.

Filing your name with your local county reporter is an easy thing to do. There is a one-page form to fill out, and a search is conducted to ensure that no one else is using the same name. There is a nominal filing fee, usually about $25, and you are then required to publish the name in any newspaper for four weeks. In addition, there are companies that do all of this for you for an additional nominal fee. Once you have your official fictitious business name, you can use that and either your tax ID number or your social security number to open a business account at the bank.

Reseller's License

One very valuable piece of paper to have is a Reseller's License. Unless you have one, vendors will insist on charging you sales tax for any items you buy from them. They are required to do so, unless you are licensed and have proof that you are purchasing those items solely for resale. This is available from your state's Department of Revenue. After acquiring your Seller's Tax Permit, you provide each vendor with a copy. You then have to fill out a Resale Exemption Certificate with each individual vendor, outlining the exact merchandise you are purchasing that is exempt from sales tax. Most vendors have copies of the certificate, and if they don't, you can acquire that from your local Department of Revenue as well.

Get a Local
Business License

At this point, you have set up your sole proprietorship or corporation, you have a business bank account, a tax ID number, and you can purchase product tax-exempt for resale. There is only one final step to take before you are officially in business. This will require a little bit of research on your part. Although you are operating on the Internet, you are treated as a home-based business and are still required to obtain a business license for the city you reside in. I may have been selling to Florida, New York, and Ohio, but I needed a license to conduct my business from Los Angeles, California. Any person operating a legitimate eBay business is required to find out what the local laws governing small businesses are in their area. This is not difficult to do, and the information is usually available on your local government's Web site.

Generally, the only thing you have to do is obtain a Local Business License or Tax Certificate. In addition, different areas have different laws and regulations governing home-based businesses. There may be special rules regarding hours of operation, shipping schedule, and the storage of inventory. Usually these are not very strict, but it is important to do your research in case you ever have a neighbor complaining about noise or activity.

Collect Tax

Right from the very beginning, I did a heck of a good job in collecting sales tax—that's one of the few "business" decisions I did well. I was excellent at it. To qualify as a home business, you must collect state sales tax on sales made within the state you live in. You do not have to charge (or collect) sales tax if you are shipping out of state. It took me over six months—and my relationship with Will—to get on the right path of sales tax remittance. You will want to do it right from the very beginning, to avoid getting yourself in trouble.

In retrospect, one mistake I made was in setting priorities. Listing more items and making more sales was a huge priority for me. Organizing my finances and researching the laws governing my business were very low on the totem pole. At some point, at the end of the day, I would sit down and wonder if we'd made any money that day. I love making sales on eBay. When you worry that your item isn't going to sell and then there's a bidding war in the last minute, the feeling is incredible. The last thing I was worried about was keeping records and remitting sales tax. My eBay sales were over $100,000 a month before I got serious about our bookkeeping. I had no bookkeeper, no financial strategist, no tax planning, and no understanding of the laws governing our business. I didn't really know what I was making, so if I had known to remit, I wouldn't have known how much.

You have to collect sales tax only from residents
of your state.

Except for printing the shipping labels, I barely knew where sales were coming from. I had to scramble to put the proper pieces together and get our business in order. Will likes to remind me that had he and I been working together from day one, he could have saved me in excess of $25,000 just by having accurate bookkeeping and tax payment programs in place from the start.

When your business grows to a certain size, the govern-
ment will notice you. There's no way to fly under the
radar. They will see your bank deposits and the income
you generate. They will come to you and demand that
you remit sales tax on every item you've sold. Whether
you've been collecting sales tax or not, you will still be
responsible for that money. You could start a thriving
business and all of a sudden be in debt to the govern-
ment for $60,000 or $70, 000. There is nothing worse
than putting your blood, sweat, and tears into building
a success only to see it all disappear because you
forgot to collect sales tax. This is, however, an easily
preventable catastrophe.

There is a common misperception among Internet buyers that any purchase made in cyberspace is exempt from sales tax. As I mentioned earlier, Internet businesses are subject to all of the same laws governing any business. If you're buying in a store, from a catalog or online, you always have to pay sales tax for any item purchased from a vendor in your home state. It is the merchant's responsibility to collect sales tax from residents of the state in which he maintains his place of business. There has been some controversy about how to determine this. I have warehouses in a number of states. My home base of operations, however, is only in California. A number of criteria have been developed to establish where the "nexus" of your business is. Where you reside, where you have an office, where you have employees, and where you store your inventory, all contribute to the determination of your nexus. For a small eBay business, this is usually a clear-cut issue, as most of your operations occur right in your living room.

Experiment

All of these steps you take to set up your eBay business are well worth the effort. A traditional brick-and-mortar store would require a significantly greater amount of time and start-up capital. Most people either take out a second mortgage on their home or risk funds from their 401(k) or other savings to realize their dream of starting their own business. They will need a bare minimum of $10,000 to $15,000 just to get their store started, with absolutely no guarantee they'll ever break even.

On eBay, this simply isn't necessary. You can begin selling tonight for $0.30. If your item doesn't sell, you can experiment with it and relist for another $0.30. A $10 or $15 investment will tell you everything you need to know. If your product is a winner, run with it. If not, use another $15 to try something else. I experimented with a pool table. The experiment was successful, but I've run others with different products, which have failed miserably. I abandoned them quickly, after a nominal investment, and moved on to others that were more profitable.

In a traditional retail environment, if the market for your product suddenly dries up, you could lose everything. You can't just switch gears midway without a considerable additional investment. You can't be in the cog business today and the space sprockets business tomorrow. Not only is it possible on eBay, but it's a typical modus operandi.

Some products last for years and others maybe a Christmas season or two. If I knew Nintendo was going to have staying power like this, I'd own an island right now. On the other hand, anyone who invested heavily in Teddy Ruxpin lost their shirt, pants, belt, and shoes, to boot. Many people don't realize the amount of capital required to keep the shelves of even a small boutique stocked with merchandise. If that merchandise doesn't sell, they can suffer huge losses. Eighty-five percent of small businesses close in their first five years, and I would guess much of that can be attributed to failure to move inventory.

The following is a typical interview for a position at my company:

ME: I see here you have a lot of experience selling pool tables.
INTERVIEWEE: Oh yes. I know everything there is

to know about pool tables. I've sold big ones, little ones, old ones, new ones. I know pool tables. I know felt, I know wood, I know pockets, I know cue sticks—I know it all. If you want someone who knows pool tables, I'm your man.

ME: Next week we may be selling garden tools.

INTERVIEWEE: Huh?

I make sure that every new employee I hire is aware that the company may change its product at any time. Today we may sell pool tables, but I don't know what we'll be selling in six, twelve, or eighteen months. The day you order inventory for your new store, you are committed to a path and a product. Open a camera store, and you're a camera salesman. You can't decide you want to add model trains to your repertoire and bring them into your camera shop. The two are inconsistent. On eBay, you can sell anything out of your store. If you get a whim to sell Wonder Woman Underoos or meet a contact who has access to a large shipment of Sea Monkeys, you can add them to your eBay store filled with first-aid kits, and no one will bat an eye. In fact, in six months you may be the largest vendor of Sea Monkeys on eBay, the first-aid kits a fond but blurry memory. This freedom and versatility is one of the elements that makes eBay such a desirable place to conduct your operations.

Low Overhead

---

*Another attractive element of an eBay business is the low
overhead it requires. If you owned that camera store, you
would have to pay rent, insurance, payroll, inventory, ad
infinitum. Many of these traditional overhead expenses do
not exist for an eBay business. This allows you to make
profit with much less volume.*

You can get started selling ten watches instead of two
hundred. You have a much lower barrier, or break-even
point, to overcome to make a profit.

You can run an eBay business without ever laying eyes
on your inventory. Via drop shipping, you can essentially be a middle man, a broker, connecting supplier, and
buyer. Although you may have product similar to that of
other eBay sellers, you can still compete successfully
using the strategies previously outlined in this book.
Drop shipping is another viable way to purchase, distrib-
ute, and ship your product. There's no need to turn your
den into a warehouse. There are suppliers just waiting to
ship straight to your customers. All you have to do is create listings and make orders. In a retail store, you have to
stock your shelves.

If you've ever dreamed of living in a hut on an island
in the Caribbean, you can do so and still run your eBay
business, as long as your hut has Internet access. Your
eBay business can be wherever in the world you want it
to be, even in a hippie van, as I mentioned in the first
chapter of the book. Most people who open a traditional

business don't go on vacation for years, not even for a weekend getaway. They are so tied to their locus of operations they simply can't leave. They either don't trust their employees to handle possible catastrophes or don't have employees to trust. eBay goes where your laptop goes. Where else but the Internet can you conduct transactions from anywhere at any time? eBay is open twenty-four hours a day, seven days a week, everywhere in the world.

I typically sell a few pool tables Christmas day. It's always prime selling time somewhere. You do not have to live a nine-to-five existence anymore. If you miss your college days, when you stayed up past four and slept until noon, you can have them again tomorrow. eBay makes all of this possible.

PowerSeller

eBay is excellent at aiding and promoting people in the community who are successful. One of the jewels in the eBay crown is its PowerSeller Program. When an eBay seller grosses a certain amount a month and maintains a minimum feedback rating of one hundred with 98 percent of that positive, they are invited to join the PowerSeller program. There are five tiers to the program—from bronze, which requires a gross of $1,000 a month, to titanium, which requires a gross of $150,000 a month. You can strive to climb the PowerSeller ladder, rung by rung, level by level.

There are benefits eBay provides to PowerSellers, including priority customer support, technical assistance for accounts, and the use of eBay online services. If a member of the general eBay community has a problem that requires eBay's help, they have to send an e-mail. A hundred and fifteen million members and counting can generate a lot of e-mail. As a PowerSeller, you have access to phone support. If you have listing issues, problems with a buyer, technical difficulties, or any other needs, that phone support is incredibly helpful. There are also health benefits, a newsletter, exclusive offers, and the support of the PowerSeller community. You'll be able to interact with other PowerSellers, develop relationships and friendships with them, and learn advanced techniques and strategies. Being a PowerSeller adds credibility to your eBay business. Every time your User ID appears on eBay, the PowerSeller logo will be displayed right along with it. Buyers will know that you are a successful and trustworthy transactioneer.

Exit Strategy

One final thing to think about as you're starting your business is an exit strategy. This is the first question Diane Kennedy asks clients when they walk in her door to discuss starting a venture. Usually they look at her like she's crazy. They're trying to figure out how to get started, and this woman wants to know what they're going to do when they're finished with it. The fact is that you're building an asset. Eventually you can sell it, turn it over to your kids when you decide to retire, or keep it as a stream of income to make other investments. It is always good to know where you're going.

Alice in Wonderland asked the Cheshire Cat which way to go when she reached the fork in the road. The Cat asked her where she was going, and she told him she didn't know. He responded, "Then it doesn't matter which road you take, does it?" If you know where you're going, you'll know the steps you need to take to get there.

It's also fun to think about how you're going to spend all this money you'll be making. You don't want to count your chickens before they hatch, but it's OK to dream about them incubating. There are two kinds of money challenges in this world. Not enough money is certainly difficult to deal with. Too much money is a fortunate challenge, but it is still a challenge. You want to invest your money wisely so that it reproduces. You might as well start thinking about what you're going to do with all this money you'll be making on eBay.

The core philosophies and system outlined in this book work on eBay. They work for any product. They work for pool tables, T-shirts, iPods, and art. If you understand the marketplace and your customer, you will be able to make a profit. eBay provides you with the opportunity to work at home, to spend more time with your family, to do whatever it is you want. This entire process, however, is like building a house. At some point, it's going to collapse if you don't first install the proper foundation. Proper bookkeeping, paying your taxes, keeping your finger on the pulse of your business so that you can make informed decisions, all make up the foundation upon which your eBay structure is built. If it is strong, there is no end to what you can do.

Growing Your Business

- Use Quickbooks Pro or other bookkeeping software to keep accurate records
- Good record keeping will keep your finger on the pulse of your business
- Consider hiring a bookkeeper to keep your books for you or to teach you how
- When you are ready to officially set up your business, hire a lawyer to help you with the legal issues and a tax strategist to help you start saving money right away
- Make sure your advisors are well-versed in Internet traffic
- Once your business expands to one hundred auctions a month, look into auction software, such as auctionit-fast.com
- Choose a business entity: usually sole proprietorship to begin with, then S-Corporation as your business grows
- Open a separate checking account
- File a fictitious business name
- Get a reseller's license
- Get a local business license
- Collect sales tax from residents of your state
- Experiment with product
- Take advantage of the PowerSeller program
- Develop an exit strategy

CHAPTER TEN

Tax Benefits

Regardless of your occupation, income, or spending habits, taxes are probably your biggest expense. By starting a home-based business, you can cut that expense dramatically. When I started selling on eBay out of my basement, I had no idea there were tax benefits created directly for people like me. I had my box of paperwork in the corner, and whichever sheet happened to be on top was the extent of my financial information I could easily put my finger on. Then I met Will, who helped me organize myself and introduced me to the financial possibilities my business offered me. Soon thereafter I met Diane Kennedy, author of *Loopholes of the Rich*, who really helped me to understand the tax benefits to owning a home-based business. She contributed her expertise to my "Fast Cash" instructional materials in addition to much of the knowledge I will impart to you now. If you'd like more information, check out her Web sites, taxloopholes.com and dkacpa.com, for free tax strategies and the latest updates in tax planning.

Words of Wisdom

"The rich buy assets. The poor only have expenses. The middle class buys liabilities they think are assets."

—*Robert Kiyosaki*, Rich Dad, Poor Dad

The most important thing Diane taught me is not some secret deduction to take but an overall philosophy. Until recently, most Americans rightly assumed that if you went to college, got a good job at a good company, and worked hard for forty years, you could count on that company to take care of you in your retirement. That plan simply doesn't work anymore. With the current economy, many people have found their 401(k) funds have been considerably diminished. Today, working harder will not make you more money. Working differently, however, will. As you invest and build assets, your bottom line will grow without you ever lifting a finger. Your money will go to work for you.

Make Money from the Start

From Diane I have learned that the simplest way to make more money is to pay less taxes.

Unfortunately, if you work for someone else and have no investments, there is very little tax planning you can do. You go to work, collect a paycheck, and the government takes its share. There's not much more to it. Owning a home-based business, however, allows you to take control of your financial future. You will be working for yourself and pay less taxes, to boot. For example, I knew a gentleman who was making $50,000 as an employee. He then went into business for himself as an independent contractor. He made the same $50,000 he had as an employee but saved an extra $10,000 in taxes, because he had his own business.

If you want to break out of your current income structure and find financial freedom, starting an eBay business is one sound possibility to consider.

If you start a small business on the side, you can still take advantage of the tax strategies outlined in this chapter while maintaining your current employment. This is especially true of an eBay business, because you can choose exactly how much time you want to devote to your new venture.

If you make an extra $200 a week, the tax benefits will actually increase that number to closer to $300.

That's an extra $15,000 a year in your pocket.

You can use your weekly paycheck to support you as you build your eBay business to the point that it can act as your main source of income. If you were starting a traditional brick-and-mortar business, you would never have the time to keep your regular job. You would also have to invest and risk a tremendous amount in start-up costs and overhead, with no guarantee of ever making your money back. You can start your eBay business with minimal risk, in your spare time, and experiment with different products and strategies until you find your formula for success. In addition, you can do all of this while reaping the same tax benefits of owning your own business.

Instead of seeing it as your enemy, you can actually make the Internal Revenue Service your partner in your new eBay business. Diane Kennedy defines tax loopholes as government incentives to promote public policy. The IRS wants you to have a home-based business, so they have created certain laws to encourage you to do so. Half of the Gross Domestic Product in the United States came from small businesses last year. Half of that came from home-based businesses. This makes them very important to our nation's economy and also quite valuable as a source of income to the IRS.

People often worry that a home-based business is like a red flag and will almost guarantee an audit. In reality, the opposite is true. The government wants you to have a business and it wants you to invest. They love when people start small businesses. They invest in equipment, they hire advisors, they may hire an employee or two, and they generate revenue. Businesses feed the economy. They want you to invest, because that feeds the economy, too.

If you make the IRS your partner by doing what they want you to do, they in turn will provide you with certain benefits. Because they want you to have a small business, the government has recently changed or created laws to make that option especially attractive. You will help the economy, and the IRS will support your effort and contribution by saving you money. This support comes in the form of a variety of tax deductions.

An eBay business qualifies for all of the same deductions as any home-based business. You will immediately be eligible for very valuable tax benefits. You will profit from the sales you make and save on taxes at the same time. In addition, you are building an asset. Your successful business will be worth something to you, your children, and possibly future generations. It may be something you can sell somewhere down the line as well. Assets are income-generators, and they will set you free.

When I realized the tax deductions I could take as a result of my eBay business, I was floored. I was able to use my savings to reinvest in my business and increase my profitability even more. It can be a never-ending cycle. You can also use your tax savings to invest in outside assets, such as real estate or other ventures. Starting with you eBay business, you can begin to build an empire.

Do You Have a Business?

Before you can take advantage of the tax strategies discussed in this chapter, you have to be able to prove that you do, indeed, have a home-based business. You do not have to make a certain amount of money or involve yourself in a certain number of transactions to do so. There are nine factors the IRS uses to determine if you have a home-based business, and using these, even the tiniest businesses can qualify.

Without your meeting these criteria, your activities on eBay will be considered a hobby instead of a business. You can still take deductions related to your hobby, but you can't deduct a loss as you would if you were running a business. It may seem counterintuitive, but a loss can actually be a good thing. If you can create a "paper loss," where you legally meet the requirements to prove your business is losing money, you can deduct that loss and offset it against your income. That is one way to pay less tax. There are many others we will discuss, but first, using the nine factors, you have to prove you have a business.

1. The first of the nine factors is probably the most important one. You must run your operation in a businesslike manner.

You have to keep good records and treat your business like a business, as opposed to a hobby. Unfortunately for me, that box in the corner was not going to cut it. Anything you do to analyze, track, and improve your business goes a long way toward proving that you treat your venture as a legitimate business. You can even use the fact that you bought this book, as it shows that you are trying to learn more about and improve your eBay business.

2. The second factor is the time and effort you put into your business.

You have to document what you do for your business, when you do it, and for how long, to show exactly what energy you are putting into your operation. Track how much time you spend listing items, corresponding with customers, shipping packages, etc. These are time-consuming tasks that will show how serious you are about your business.

3. **The next criterion relates to your income. You do not have to be dependent on your business as your main source of income when you are starting out, but you at least need a plan that someday you will be.**

You have to be able to show that you intend on quitting your day job at some point in the future to focus entirely on your eBay business. Writing out a simple business plan should be sufficient for this criterion.

4. **If you have losses, the fourth factor states that you are doing something reasonable to change that.**

Most businesses, small and large, suffer losses in the beginning. This is expected, and you will not be penalized for it. The key is that you are trying to reverse the situation and make a profit.

5. **The fifth element on the list is that you have to make a concerted effort to generate profit.**

This may seem obvious, but you have to be able to prove that you are not lackadaisical about your business. If something isn't working, you have to show that you are making a change. Going to seminars, studying your marketplace, trying different strategies, and meeting with advisors are all ways to actually prove you are trying to make money. Simply saying, "Well, of course I am really trying to make a profit," will not suffice.

6. **Hiring and meeting with experienced advisors is the sixth factor the IRS will look at.**

They want you to capitalize on the knowledge of professionals who understand eBay, small businesses, bookkeeping, and the marketplace and economy. Small businesses fail at an incredible rate. The IRS correctly believes that relying on experienced advisors will not only help you avoid failure but actually help you ensure success. The sole purpose of this rule is the IRS wants you to do well. They have a vested interest in the success of your business, because they make money whenever you do. They want you to get rich. Nothing would make them happier than to see your business become a powerhouse.

7. **The seventh element the IRS looks at is your experience level. If you have no experience in the arena you are working in, you have to show that you are working to gain experience.**

Again, learning, buying books, working with advisors, all help in this area. Anything you do to show you are trying to become an expert in your field will satisfy the requirements of this element. Experience, too, helps determine your success. The IRS wants a competent partner they can put their faith in.

8. **The eighth factor is a continuation of the fifth. First you had to prove you were trying your best to make a profit. Now you have to show that you've had profit in the past, are generating profit now, or reasonably expect profit in the future.**

At some point, your business has to make money to be a business. I'm sure that you and the IRS are together on this one.

9. **The final criterion on the list is that your business is an asset that is appreciating.**

Many people don't think about it, but besides creating cash flow and tax deductions, a business is actually an asset. It is something of value that you can sell or pass down as a legacy to your heirs. The IRS wants to see that you are building an entity you expect will be worth something someday.

You do not have to meet all of these criteria to qualify as a small business. When you are starting out, you are not necessarily going to have every detail in place. You may not have hired advisors yet. You may not be making a profit. You must simply show that you are reasonably working toward these things. The fundamental element is the first. If you are running your operation in a businesslike manner, everything else will fall into place. Keep good records, copies of receipts, and proof that you are trying to collect on accounts receivable. These are all good evidence that you do, indeed, have a business.

Keep Track

As you can see from the nine factors defining a business, the key is good record keeping. As long as you do what the IRS wants you to do and have the documentation to prove it, they will gladly throw juicy tax benefits at you. As I discussed in the previous chapter, proper bookkeeping will benefit you not only in regard to taxes but in regard to your overall business. You will be able to see what is and is not working, and make informed decisions that improve your bottom line.

Good record keeping is not an impossible task. A decent filing system so you can find things, and well-kept Quickbooks data are all you will need. If you set everything up and organize yourself properly from the beginning, maintaining your system will be relatively simple. There are two very important details to track in the course of your eBay business. The first is the winning bids of your auctions and who your successful bidders are. This will tell you which items are selling and for what kind of profit margin. You can also begin to build a customer database and track your repeat business. The second thing to keep track of is your money flow, both incoming and outgoing. If you accept PayPal and use it to pay your seller's fees, PayPal will provide you with all of your information in a clear, comprehensive manner.

Good record keeping will allow you to sleep at night.

If perchance you are selected for an audit, you won't have anything to worry about, because you will have all the evidence you need to prove you have been conducting your affairs properly. People who try to scam the government generally get caught. With all of the incentives the IRS offers you, there is no reason to even attempt it. Keep good records, report everything, and take advantage of all the tax loopholes you possibly can.

The secret to truly reaping the benefits of all of these tax loopholes is not to go out and spend money you don't have. Instead, learn to turn things you already spend money on into legitimate business deductions. Almost anything you use in the course of your business can be deducted, even if they are personal items. You probably already pay for a cell phone, a car, and a place to live. Because you also need them to run your business, you can deduct at least a portion of them from your income taxes. Think about everything you currently spend money on. If it can help your business, you can deduct it. The best course of action is to hire an accountant to help you determine what will and won't qualify for a deduction. There are nuances in the tax laws, and they will understand them inside and out.

Home Deduction

One of the biggest and most helpful deductions your home-based business is now eligible for is your actual home, or at least a portion thereof. You can deduct whatever percentage of your home you dedicate to your home office. Assume you have a thousand-square-foot, two-bedroom home. If you use one two-hundred-square-foot bedroom as your eBay office, you have dedicated twenty percent of your home to your business.

You can now deduct 20 percent of your rent or mortgage, 20 percent of your property tax, 20 percent of your utilities, 20 percent of your insurance, etc.

For someone earning W2 income, this can mean an immediate deduction of $5,000 before they've made a penny on eBay. This deduction is relatively new. For many years, a home office was viewed as a residence and therefore ineligible for the deductions granted to traditional places of business. Tax law has changed, however, and if you are doing business out of your home, you may deduct a portion of your home. Just because you live there doesn't mean you don't also conduct your affairs there.

In addition to a percentage of your home expenses, everything in your office is deductible. The business is using your desk, the chair you pulled out of your attic, your brand-new computer. All of these things have value, and the business has to pay you back for them.

Quick Tip

> Your Internet service, your phone, and your printer are all deductible.

Whatever it takes to make your business run can be written off. If you've already paid for many of these things and are just transferring them to the business, you are essentially getting free money from the government.

On top of all of these deductions, you also save the money you would have spent on an outside office or store. You have to live somewhere, but now you can deduct part of that. You don't, however, have to spend the hundreds or thousands of dollars in rent to maintain a brick-and-mortar location. You would typically pay about $1,500 in rent for a thousand square feet of retail space. That $1,500 you'd be saving is enough to hire an employee or pay for any number of business expenses. The savings are huge when you add to rent the displays, furniture, fixtures, and other expenses required of a physical location. With a home-based business, you save in taxes and all of these other expenses. The difference is extreme.

The rules regarding this benefit are very clear. There

are only two things you need to do in order to prove you have a home-based office and take this valuable deduction. First, you must have a space in your home that is exclusively for business use. If you conduct your affairs with your iBook in your lap from your living-room couch or at your dining-room table, you will not be able to claim this deduction. I worked from my otherwise unused basement and was able to take advantage. A spare bedroom, a loft, even a corner of a room, will qualify as long as you dedicate the space to your business and use it for nothing else. After dedicating a space, you must then regularly conduct some kind of business there. With an eBay business, this is easy to prove, because your computer is there. You do so much of your work on your computer that there is no doubt where you spend your time.

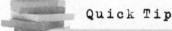

Quick Tip

One of the best ways to prove you have a legitimate home office is to take a picture.

Diane Kennedy had a client with a home-based business who was selected for an audit. She went to the audit to represent her client, and there was a list of things the auditor wanted to investigate. Diane started off by saying, "Why don't we just deal with the home office first?" The auditor had a gleam in her eye, as the home office is generally a difficult element to prove. Thinking she would nail them on the first element, the auditor eagerly agreed. Diane opened her file folder and pulled out a photograph.

> *The auditor looked at the picture for a moment and*
> *then said, "We're done."*

She stopped the audit. After everything was signed and sealed, Diane asked the auditor why she had let them go so easily. The auditor responded, "You know, I knew you had good records, I could see by all the files you brought in, but when you showed me that picture, that was so over the top, I knew that we were done then. We didn't need to do anything further." So, a picture can be worth a thousand words, or a thousand dollars, in this case.

Automobile Deduction

Someone who works outside of their home cannot usually deduct much of their automobile expenses. The miles they travel from their home to their place of business are considered a commute and not eligible for deduction. There are people who live in San Diego who commute to Los Angeles. They drive one hundred miles each way, five days a week, fifty weeks a year. That's fifty thousand miles traveled for work that are completely ineligible for deduction, according to the IRS. Apparently, they do not want you to commute long distances.

With a home-based business, your commute is your

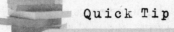

Quick Tip

Once you arrive at work, however, any traveling you do in the scope of employment is deductible.

slippered stroll from your bedroom to your spare bedroom, or den, or basement, whatever the case may be. Then, in the course of the day, any driving you do for your business can be deducted. If you go out to pick up inventory or office supplies, that's deductible. If you go to the post office to ship items, that's deductible. You can even deduct a trip to the mall if you use it to do research as to the product available. Anything that can be couched in a business capacity is a legitimate write-off. Additionally, vacations are deductible if you can frame them as a business trip as well.

There are three different ways you can take an auto deduction. The first way is to claim a certain number of cents per mile. This number is currently 37.5 cents, but it changes every year, sometimes even twice a year. You can check the IRS Web site, irs.org, for current rates. If you have an older, low-value vehicle you put a lot of miles into, this option is probably the best for you.

The second auto deduction to choose from is Diane Kennedy's favorite loophole of all. This is the Heavy Vehicle deduction and applies to any vehicle you purchase over six thousand GVW (Gross Vehicle Weight). This includes SUVs, big four-by-four trucks, and other large vehicles. If you purchase one of these, you can immediately take a write-off of up to $100,000. Often dealerships offer specials where you can buy a car for 0 percent down and 0 percent interest. You drive away with a brand-new car for nothing initially but can immediately deduct 100 percent of the value. You can then invest that money, so that by the time you pay for the car, it's actually earned you a profit. Of course, you may end up paying more in gas than you'd ever thought possible, but it is a deduction to consider nonetheless.

The final option involves luxury cars. If this is the kind of car you own or intend on owning, you may want to consider leasing instead of buying. You will generally be able to deduct more with a lease of a luxury car than a purchase. The best thing to do in any of these cases is to meet with an advisor and discuss all three scenarios. The question is not "Should I deduct my auto?" but "How?" The IRS wants you to take advantage of these benefits, and your advisor will help you to determine the best course of action to do so.

The auto deduction is a huge benefit to running a home-based business. If you worked elsewhere, you would probably not be able to take it.

This is yet another area, however, where you must keep proper records. The government will want to see proof that you use your automobile in a business capacity. It is Diane's recommendation that you keep a log for two or three months, documenting all of your mileage, both business and personal. With this information, you can determine exactly what percentage of your auto use is business-related.

Deduct Your Family!

Believe it or not, you can deduct your family.

Kids are an enormous expense in this world. In addition to feeding, clothing, and schooling them, there are also summer camps, class trips, Game Boys, birthday parties, ad infinitum. Instead of giving your kids an allowance, put them to work, and you can deduct them as employees. There are a number of things they can do to assist an eBay business. They can learn the Internet or, what is more likely, teach you the Internet by helping with listings. You can teach them to help with filing and record keeping. You can teach them to help with sales and marketing strategies. These are skills that will come in handy and help them succeed throughout their lives.

While you're providing them this valuable education, you can also pay them a salary, which you can deduct.

If you pay them around $4,900 (this number changes from year to year, too, so check irs.org for current figures), and they have no other source of income, they will not have to pay income tax. You will still be able to claim them as dependents. You can save about $1,500 a year just by putting your kids to work. Don't pay them an allowance—pay them a wage. You can use this opportunity to teach them about managing their money and paying expenses, or you can use that money to save for their education. You will now do something all parents should strive for: pay for college with pretax money.

You can even put your youngest children to work. If you're selling baby clothes, toys, or something similar, you can use your children as models for your listing photographs and pay them a fee for their services. Be creative but legitimate. You can use your kids for product testing. If you're selling toys, I'm sure they'd love to make money trying out new items and telling you what they think of them. Make sure, however, that the information they provide is useful to your business, and document the time and effort they contribute.

You don't have to focus solely on your kids. You can put your spouse to work. Even if they have a full-time job, you can hire them part-time and claim them as a deduction. You can hire your mother in Long Island, your nephew Ari in Miami Beach, your cousin Rachel in Seattle. Because you are running an Internet-based company, work for it can be conducted from anywhere. They can post listings, correspond with customers, conduct your bookkeeping, and so on, from any place on the planet with an Internet connection. You can put your family members to work and deduct them as you would any employees. Often, we don't feel comfortable bringing strangers into our homes as employees. This is a perfect way to rely on family and save money at the same time.

401(k)

In 2001 the IRS introduced a great new benefit for sole proprietors. This is the solo 401(k) plan. Before this plan, sole proprietors had to have a certain number of employees before they could put a significant amount of their earnings into savings. There were no provisions for the mom-and-pop or one-person businesses to open a 401(k).

Now you can put up to $13,000 dollars a year into your own 401(k) plan. This allows you to reap the same benefits as employees and owners of much larger companies.

Health Insurance

If you are self-employed, you can now deduct 100 percent of your health insurance.

This is a tremendous savings, as health insurance is so expensive. This law was put into effect in 2003. As of January 2004, you can now open a Health Care Savings Account. Many people have high-deductible health insurance, because they can't afford a lower-deductible HMO plan. Those people can now open a Health Care Savings Account, which works like an IRA. You are allowed to put pretax money into the account. The interest you earn on it is tax-free, as are any withdrawals you make, as long as they are medically related. This includes dental care, going to a chiropractor, doctor's visits, prescriptions, and so on. Health Care Savings Accounts are now flexible. Previously, if you did not use the funds in the account by the end of the fiscal year, they were no longer available to you. Now they build and accumulate over time. These benefits are incredibly useful to small-business owners, who previously had access to no health care benefits at all.

Accelerated Depreciation

One of the significant expenses for your eBay business will be your computer. With modern technology improving so rapidly, computers are outdated usually by the time you get the box into the car. I replace my laptop about every two years.

> *As of 2003, you can deduct a larger percentage of busi-*
> *· ness purchases that depreciate in the first year.*

Before 2003, you had to spread purchase deductions over several years. You might still be deducting a computer after you had replaced it twice. Now, with Accelerated Depreciation, you can deduct a much larger portion upfront.

You may consider passing along some of your savings to your customers in the form of discounts. This will allow you to compete successfully with sellers who have overhead. Many big companies are selling on eBay, but they have to pay for all the infrastructure their organizations need to operate. They have to pay salaries, rent, vendors, ad infinitum. You can sell the exact same product for less, because you're working out of your house and enjoying similar tax benefits.

> *The brilliant thing about an eBay business is that you can*
> *take advantage of all these deductions and keep working*
> *at your current job, if you so desire. If you have a home*
> *business, you will have more money in your pocket than a*
> *coworker making the exact same salary, even if your busi-*
> *ness is losing money. You will be able to write off part of*
> *your home, part of your car, part of your travel, even part*
> *of your kids. Pretax dollars will now pay for expenses you*
> *already had. The bottom line is, you will pay less taxes*
> *and have more money in your bank account.*

Just being an employee simply doesn't cut it anymore when it comes to financial planning, especially in regard to taxes. It is time to start thinking, "How can I do things differently?" These strategies apply both to someone who's just starting out and to the most advanced Titanium PowerSeller. If you start an eBay business or any home-based business, you can save yourself an enormous amount in tax write-offs before you've even made your first sale. As long as you're attempting to establish your venture according to the nine factors, in the eyes of the Internal Revenue Service, you have a business. I hope I have introduced you to not only some very specific strategies for running an eBay business but also a new way of thinking, which will help increase your bottom line for years to come.

*** *I would highly encourage you to hire a local tax specialist in your area. You can also contact Tax Loopholes as an alternative. The information contained in this chapter is not intended to be a substitute for hiring a tax specialist. I impart to you the concepts I have learned from tax experts over the years although I would certainly not consider myself a tax specialist.* ***

Make the IRS Your Partner

- Make sure your business is a legitimate business, according to IRS criteria
- Keep good records!
- Deduct part of your home, car, family, and health insurance
- Start a solo 401(k) plan
- Look into purchases that qualify for accelerated depreciation

CHAPTER ELEVEN

Tips, Tricks, and Advanced Techniques

eBay's capabilities as a market platform are continually expanding, as are the strategies you can employ to take advantage of that platform. This presents a remarkable opportunity for anyone starting an eBay business. As the technology surrounding the Internet and its applications advances, so does your business. eBay is constantly adding features and facilities you can use to increase your efficiency as a seller, improve the service you provide, and distinguish yourself from your competition. It is a good idea to closely monitor any new features eBay introduces and consider how you can incorporate them into your business structure. In this chapter, I will discuss some of the advanced techniques you can make use of today in your eBay ventures.

eBay Stores

As you grow your business, one of the best ways to increase your presence on eBay is by opening an eBay store.

For someone selling in quantity, this is an amazing feature. An eBay store is very similar to an independent-commerce Web site, with one huge advantage—visibility. Running your own commerce site is like setting claim to an island in the middle of the vast Internet sea. If you're lucky and clever enough, hits to your Web site might trickle in as passersby happen upon your "island" through one of the many search engines out there. Running an eBay store, on the other hand, gives you instant access to eBay's 115 million and counting customers.

Suddenly, your business is smack in the middle of the busiest shopping district on the Internet.

Unlike owning a store in a busy shopping district, the rent on your eBay store is dirt-cheap. The cost of starting and maintaining an eBay store is currently $10 a month. This is practically nothing compared to the costs of running an independent Web site. Hosting is included, which pays for the eBay store fee in a single sweep. You don't need to spend money on a design team or worry about a payment gateway, either. The entire eBay infrastructure is made available to you with your store.

Your Store's Look and Feel

The design of your store is a critical component of your overall business strategy and, more specifically, your brand strategy.

As of recently, eBay has amended its policy that once limited your store's appearance to a one-style-fits-all template. Listening to the suggestions of thousands of store owners, eBay now allows free-form usage of HTML, so you can design your store any way you like. If you don't know HTML, and don't have the time or the techy-inclination to learn it, zTemplates will create your eBay store for you, just as it does with your listings. zTemplates will pair you with one of their Web designers and they will provide a logo and a look-and-feel to your store, which represents your business professionally, stylishly, and in accordance with your overall brand strategy. They will even help you develop a brand strategy and design theme if you haven't already thought about it. Developing and executing a brand strategy can be one of a starting business's single largest, and most necessary, expenses. Together with its listing design service, zTemplates ensures that your store and your brand will be everything you want them to be but are afraid to do yourself or pay professionals to do for you.

Save Big on Listing Fees

Another huge benefit to the eBay store is that the listing fees are substantially lower than in regular eBay auctions.

Quick Tip

Each item you list in your store will cost you only $0.02 for thirty days, regardless of an item's starting price.

On eBay itself, you would currently pay somewhere between $0.03 and $4.80 for the exact same item. It is an inexpensive way to list many items at once. If you're selling in large volume, you can save your business hundreds and even thousands of dollars in overhead. This is a strategy you cannot afford to ignore.

Store Strategy

There are no auctions in eBay stores. Every item you sell through your store is in the fixed-price format. The items you offer in your store will also not appear when someone conducts a general keyword search on the eBay site. This turns out not to be a problem. There will be a note at the bottom of the search page, informing the buyer that there are additional items available in eBay stores, and the link will take them there if they so desire. What's more, as long as you still run traditional auctions, you can use those listings to drive people to your eBay store. Say, Jorge in Miami Beach is searching for a Stetson Panama straw hat and types in those words in the keyword search. Brock sells hats out of Denver and has a couple of Panama hats on auction, as well as hundreds more available in his store. Jorge clicks on one of Brock's listings and immediately sees that Brock has an eBay store full of Stetson hats, with dozens of Panama straw hats to choose from. Jorge visits his store, sees a straw hat that's perfect for driving around sunny Miami, and purchases it right away. When Jorge's pal Stephen compliments him on the hat, Jorge can refer him directly to Brock's eBay store. And when Jorge's hat flies off his head and out of his brand-new Volvo convertible onto the pavement on Collins Avenue, Jorge knows exactly where to go to find a replacement. Brock has made a repeat customer out of Jorge, and all of Jorge's envious sunburnt friends, and his eBay store has made it possible.

For every item that you sell in multiple quantities, you should always have at least one or two similar items available at auction at any given time, so that someone running a traditional search for it on eBay will find it.

Howard, my father-in-law, still runs traditional auctions with our zWatches User ID even though he also has a store. He posts a few high-profile auctions of the most popular watches with no reserves and low starting bids, to generate excitement and a lot of bidding activity. In the body of his listings, he has a link to the zWatches store, inviting people to see what else he has to offer. If the item for sale is a Citizen, for example, the link will say, "To see every model Citizen makes, click here." Only one person can win an auction. Many of the other bidders still want to buy a watch, so they'll go to the eBay store. Most of our products will be listed in the store, where the fees are inexpensive, with a few auctions running simultaneously, that are essentially serving as advertising tools for the zWatches store. Before eBay stores, Howard was paying around $10,000 a month in listing fees for zWatches. With the creation of the store, that number has been brought down to about $2,500. And sales have increased!

You can also treat your eBay store just as you would any Web site, and advertise it in more traditional ways. If you purchase or already own an outside domain name, you can use it to direct traffic to your eBay store. You can advertise your Web site in a variety of ways. It is, however, merely a front for your eBay store and activities. For example, if you are running a special, you may take out a newspaper ad using your URL. When customers type it into their Web browser, they are automatically directed to your eBay store (if you set it up that way). You can advertise your eBay store just as you would any other—in the Yellow Pages, in print media, flyers, radio, ad infinitum.

There is an additional bonus to doing your own advertising and using outside means to create traffic for your eBay store. If you spend your own money and don't make use of eBay's infrastructure to find customers, eBay will refund half of your fees back to you. They can easily see how a person arrived at your listing, and if it wasn't through eBay, they return 50 percent of your fees. They do this because you invested your own time and money to get customers to eBay, thereby increasing eBay's own membership and traffic. If you bring customers to your listings, they will likely stick around and check out the rest of the site. Your new customer becomes a new eBay customer, too.

Many people also search primarily within the eBay stores because they prefer a fixed-price format. They may feel more comfortable buying from someone they know has established an official presence. Even if you are working alone from home in your Spiderman pajamas, an eBay store gives the impression of a much larger business. So, in addition to the traffic you get from advertising and your other auctions, you will also get customers from the general eBay community who like the eBay store concept even more than traditional auctions.

If you already have a brick-and-mortar retail store, there is an additional benefit to maintaining a store on eBay. When you purchase inventory for your existing store, you probably get a volume discount when you buy more than a certain amount. Often, that amount is large enough that you might worry about being able to sell it all. You can use an eBay store to sell off your remaining inventory, taking advantage of that volume discount. That is pretty much how I started my own business on eBay. If you would normally buy a thousand units of an item, but there's a 10 percent discount for fifteen hundred, buy the extra five hundred and sell them in your eBay store. You have an outlet to sell excess inventory while getting an overall discount on everything you buy.

If you find, as I did, that you're pulling in more revenue on eBay than you are at your physical store location, you could start increasing the amount you order from your inventory source and take advantage of even greater volume discounts. Or, as I did, you could move your entire business onto eBay and be done with your store's rent payments. It all depends on how comfortable you get with the eBay environment and how you weigh the costs and benefits of keeping your brick-and-mortar store running. You might like the idea of keeping both sales channels available to you, perhaps even handing over the daily operations of your store to a trusted partner while you focus on the eBay market. A healthy combination of following your heart and your business brain, taking into consideration the current and future sales outlook at your retail store, comparing these to your eBay business over a period of time, and taking your lifestyle values into account, will make your move to eBay a smooth transition.

Even if you don't have a brick-and-mortar store, you can use this shared inventory concept with the product you sell on eBay. Anything you don't sell in traditional auctions you can move to your eBay store, giving them more time to sell and cheaper listing fees. eBay stores present a great opportunity for anyone serious about using the Web site as a significant source of income.

Keyword Banner Program

One of the most underutilized features on eBay is the keyword banner program. As I discussed earlier in the book, if you conduct a search on eBay, items are listed in order of those auctions ending soonest. You cannot do anything else to give your listing priority over anyone else's except for a pricey $19.95 featured-item listing, which is another option offered to you when you sell an item. Because of this, most bidding activity happens in the last few hours of your auction, as that is when your listing shows up on the first search page. This is the time when people can immediately eye your listing without having to delve deeper into the search results. The keyword banner program is the only way to get around this. In addition to the auctions listed in order of those ending soonest, search pages have advertisement banners at the top related to the items therein.

If you search for pool tables right now, there is a good chance you will see a banner advertising LasVegasTables at the top of the page. When a buyer sees the banner and clicks on it, they are taken away from the search page, effectively bypassing all of our competition, and directed straight to our eBay store. There, instead of one individual auction, they'll see all of the offerings that are currently available. The banner we run is attractive, advertising some of the perks of buying from us, such as free shipping and large selections. We designed it to be enticing enough to draw customers away from the main listing page, and thus away from any auctions run by anyone but us. This is perhaps the most powerful form of advertising available on the Internet, and since this advertising method is used all over the Internet today, it has been tried and tested by countless other businesses. The verdict is unanimous—keyword banner programs work.

The keyword banner program on eBay is free. That is, of course, until someone clicks on it. You pay for each person who clicks on your banner, so, essentially, you're paying only for true potential customers. Very few people will waste their time clicking on a banner they have absolutely no interest in. For the most part, we are going to reach only people who are seriously considering buying a pool table. They may not purchase from us, but it is certainly worth the price per click to get them into our virtual store.

Rather appropriate for eBay, pricing for the eBay banner program is determined through auction. For any specific keyword or group of keywords, you bid whatever amount you wish to pay per click. The final value is usually determined by the popularity the item has on eBay. Pool tables are not as prevalent as many other items, so the per-click rate is about $0.12. "Rolex" is an incredibly popular search word, so the price per click is much higher, at about $0.90. Rolexes can cost $12,000, however, so $0.90 per click is not an outrageous figure.

When you bid for a keyword banner, you enter the maximum you're willing to pay per click for a certain keyword, and your overall budget. Your priority of placement will depend on how high your bid is. The top three bidders' ads will be placed in a regular rotation, so you have to bid high enough for your banner to get displayed. If you have the highest bid, your ad will appear more often and at peak times. Your overall budget determines how long your keyword banner campaign will last. If you bid $0.20 a click and determine an overall budget of $20, the ad will be shown until one hundred people have clicked on your banner. You will then be asked if you wish to continue your campaign or not.

I have had great success with the keyword banner program. Statistically, it has been proven that a certain percentage of people who click actually do make a purchase. One $1,500 pool table goes a long way toward paying for all those $0.12 clicks. As an advertising tool, the keyword banner packs a lot of value into a very low cost. It is a phenomenal way to drive business to your listings and/or eBay store. Easy to use and highly effective; I definitely recommend taking advantage of it. If you want to investigate this opportunity further, go to ebaykeyword.com. If you go there, you might notice that eBay has published a testimonial I wrote about the keyword banners. I'm always happy to sing the praises of any eBay service that profits my business, because if it works for me, it can work for anyone. It goes back to a variation on the sales philosophy I spoke of earlier: the more successful people become on eBay, the more successful people will become on eBay. If there's a program out there that can help the success of an eBay business, I want to make sure people know about it.

Second-chance Offers

eBay is constantly adding tools to help its members increase sales. One technique they've recently introduced is the second-chance offer. This is an incredible opportunity to sell multiple quantities of the same item. The second-chance offer was initially designed for sellers with non-paying bidders. If the winner of the auction failed to pay, as sometimes happens, the seller would be able to offer the item to the second highest bidder at their highest bid. I have found that, used for this purpose, second-chance offers don't work very well.

By the time you realize a buyer is not going to pay, it is usually too late to go to the second highest bidder. They have probably already moved on and found the item elsewhere.

If the item is rare or one-of-a-kind, the second-chance offer may still work in this type of situation, because the second highest bidder probably has not found another like item to purchase. In general, however, I don't find these offers that effective in a non-paying bidder scenario.

The second-chance offer is a highly effective alternative, however, when you have multiples of the same item to sell.

---

eBay allows you to sell to both the highest bidder and the second highest bidder in an auction, as long as you charge each of them the price of their highest bid.

I sold a pool table at an auction for $1,400. The second highest bidder bid $1,375 and was outbid in the final minute of the auction. If I'm willing to sell the pool table for $1,400, why wouldn't I also be willing to sell it for $1,375? Twenty-five dollars isn't much of a difference. The auction started at a penny with no reserve, it certainly could have ended for a lot less than $1,375. In essence, the second highest bidder gets to buy the item for less than the winner of the auction, and you get to sell two items instead of one, using the same listing.

When you make a second-chance offer, there's no listing fee for the second item. There is absolutely no risk to the seller in making the offer. If they accept the offer and you make the sale, you do have to pay a final-value fee, but you've saved the time and effort required to post an additional auction, and you've saved yourself a listing fee. Second-chance offers work a high percentage of the time. I have found from my research that statistically as many as 20 percent of the buyers receiving second-chance offers will act on them. Without increasing my listing fees, I can make 20 percent more sales using second-chance offers.

For the greatest effect, I recommend making your second-chance offers within minutes of the auction's end.

It will arrive in the buyer's e-mail inbox in the form of a private Buy It Now auction. It will not appear in the auction listings, and there will be no further bidding on it. You can still choose, however, between a one-, three-, five-, or seven-day offer. I always offer second chances for only one day. It is best to give the buyer a sense of urgency so they feel the need to buy immediately, while you still have their attention. They were bidding on your item, and you want to maintain that momentum. You want to capitalize on that sense of ownership they had built and the frustration they're now feeling at getting outbid. You don't want to give them the chance to go out and find your item elsewhere. You'll find that most acceptances of second-chance offers happen almost immediately. The person is usually online, because they were tracking the progress of the original auction. They still have the taste of ownership in their mouth, and this is when they are most willing to jump at the chance of regaining their property. This key strategy gives you the opportunity to significantly increase your business with virtually no effort.

Three simple clicks of your mouse will lead to a second-chance offer. Once the auction concludes, you will see a link that says, "Second-chance offer." Click on that and you will see a list of your bidders and how much they bid. You highlight the highest one, which is actually your second-highest bidder, and then click on the button that says, "Submit second-chance offer." Then you're done. That's all there is to it. A thirty-second process can double your sales for any given auction.

About Me

The About Me page is your opportunity to showcase your business and tell your story on eBay. You can let your customers know who you are. You can even brag about yourself—don't be shy. It is also the only place on eBay where you can include links to outside Web sites. If you have a Web site you've set up to promote your business, you can advertise it on your About Me page.

For me, the About Me page is a landing place for all of my outside advertising. I mentioned earlier that when I advertise pool tables, I provide a URL that forwards directly to my About Me page. When people type in that URL, it takes them to my About Me page. There they will see all the specials I'm running and all the products I have for sale. It is a virtual hub for my business, where a buyer can browse my offerings and then be redirected straight to either my listings or to my eBay store. They can also see information about my business—who I am and what I'm all about. It's professional, it's clean, and it's consistent with the look of our listings. The About Me page is home base for building and maintaining your brand.

You can have your About Me page designed professionally or you can do it yourself, using eBay's About Me template builder, which is, like most things on eBay, very simple to use. You can also use zTemplates to tailor your page to your exact specifications and match the design to that of your listings and your store. The About Me page is entirely customizable. It gives you room for flexibility and allows you to do things that aren't possible in the body of your listings. This feature is really as much an "About Me" page as it is an "About Them" page, "them" referring to my potential customers. It is as much about my business as it is about the customer and the excitement I want to create in them. I try to show them how they can take advantage of the quality and service I provide and how they can't miss out on the opportunities being presented to them.

The About Me page is great if you're selling a variety of items. You can feature all of your categories, showing off everything you have available. This will give the impression that you are a large retailer with an array of product and a large inventory. Within each category, you will include all of your individual auctions, driving people directly to your listings. A categorized listing of your items can be done with little effort, either using zTemplates or the HTML editor that eBay provides when you're creating your About Me page. If you choose to do it yourself, then within the HTML editor area you can find a link to eBay-specific HTML tags, some of which are geared toward displaying your feedback comments and others toward displaying your current and past auctions. There are examples on that page showing

you what these HTML tags will look like on your finished About Me page. Everyone, from eBay hobbyists to
serious entrepreneurs, should take advantage of the
About Me page. It is a free-for-all promotional tool that
is, unfortunately, underrated and underutilized in the
eBay community. Most of the top sellers have spent a
great deal of time and effort creating dynamic and effective About Me pages, but you don't have to be a top seller to make use of this incredible resource. eBay doesn't
charge a dime for it, there's no monthly hosting fee, and
it can only help improve your business, your brand, and
your bottom line.

The concept to keep in mind as you get started is

---

experiment, experiment, experiment.

Have fun and play around with some of the features
eBay has to offer. You'll win and you'll lose, but you'll
gain an understanding of the marketplace and where
your business fits into it. An eBay business, by its very
nature, gives you the ability to continually revise and
improve your techniques and strategies, because implementing them requires very little investment. It is ok if
you don't always make the most on the sale. It is ok if you

Words of Wisdom

"The man who has no imagination has no wings."
—*Mohammad Ali*

don't make the sale at all or if you even lose a few dollars while you're experimenting. The end result will be forward-looking: the growth of your business and the coinciding growth of your revenue. Always thinking about what else you can do, what you can change, what you can do better, will set you apart from the competition and help you find the success you're seeking.

Advanced Tips and Techniques

- Open an eBay store
- Design your store to broadcast your brand
- Use traditional auctions to advertise your store
- Get an outside Web site and advertise it outside of eBay to drive traffic to your store
- Make use of the Keyword Banner Program
- Try your hand at second-chance offers
- Create an About Me page
- Keep abreast of new eBay features
- Always experiment and think outside the box
- Always be on the lookout for new ways to improve your business

Epilogue

I started selling on eBay for fun or, more accurately, to get my mother off my back, with no additional objectives or expectations. Now my passion is to share this information with as many people as possible. There is no better feeilng than to see someone become empowered and succeed. It is amazing how clear the world gets once you set a goal. Imagine having a map with a number of roads all crisscrossing and no towns or even rest stops. You can go forever and never arrive at your destination.

As Yogi Berra once said, "If you don't know where you're going, you'll probably end up somewhere else."

As soon as I realized what this eBay thing actually had to offer, I decided I wanted to share my knowledge with others. eBay is a dream-making machine, a democratizing power for good that can change lives with a few clicks of a mouse. I wanted to shout what I learned from the rooftops. So I began speaking and giving seminars. The Fast Cash products were developed to further help people who wanted to start their eBay businesses.

Here is a marketplace where a first-time seller can

compete with billion-dollar corporations on an equal playing field. Someone who has never even thought about starting a business can get started tonight for $0.30. Low start-up costs and overhead almost completely reduce the risk of starting an enterprise. Whereas a brick-and-mortar store could require hundreds of thousands of dollars in investment capital before the first sale is made, an eBay business can be launched for less than a dollar. Because the risk is so low, eBay allows for extensive experimentation. If one product doesn't sell, an eBayer can move on to the next, with little or no repercussions. Tax benefits for a home-based eBay business are worth thousands before a first sale is even made.

eBay allows for part-time or full-time participation. A casual seller can keep their nine-to-five job while building their eBay business on the side. They can rely on the security of a regular salary until eBay can support them completely, or they can dive right in, devoting themselves fully to their new enterprise. An eBay business can be run from anywhere and everywhere. If Internet access is available in a fishing village in Cambodia, then that village may be home to the next eBay Titanium PowerSeller. eBay is open twenty-four hours a day, seven days a week, in every corner of the earth. One hundred fifteen million customers and counting await each and every seller. eBay allows for any schedule, any seller, any dream. The potential it holds is limitless.

With all these benefits, I don't understand why anyone with the drive wouldn't start their own eBay business. This is the greatest business opportunity ever, and there isn't a single person who can't take advantage. eBay is the future of the global economy. This is why I wrote this book and why I speak to people all over this country.

A little while ago, I went to Canada with a colleague to give a seminar about eBay. We landed in Calgary, picked up a giant Yukon SUV, and set out for Edmonton, where we were speaking. It was one o'clock in the morning. It was freezing outside. We were going sixty miles an hour when we hit a patch of black ice. The Yukon spun around twice, went sideways off a six-foot ditch, and we landed in an embankment of trees. We were fine, but I can't say the same for the rental car. The Yukon was totaled.

The policeman who arrived at the scene was not amused. I suppose he was angry about having to head out to the middle of nowhere in the wee hours of the morning in the freezing cold, and he definitely intended to take his anger out on us. He put my colleague into the police car and wanted to arrest him for reckless driving. He said we were going way too fast for the current weather conditions. "There's a lot of black ice on the road here. What were you thinking?"

"What's black ice?" My colleague is from San Diego and had never even heard of it before.

The policeman was suspicious of us and wanted to know where we were going so late at night. I told him we were headed for Edmonton.

"I have to speak at ten in the morning. I'm teaching people how to sell on eBay," I explained to the officer.

His eyes lit up and his entire demeanor changed. He got excited and exclaimed, "eBay!" I'm somewhere in Canada, freezing my butt off, it's one in the morning, just had the scariest car crash of my life, my buddy is sitting inside a police car waiting to be arrested, and the cop says, "eBay! I've got twenty-one feedbacks." He gets in the car with me and continues, "I have a question for you about PayPal."

We talked for twenty minutes, with my colleague sitting in the cop car the whole time. He was agonizing over his fate and had no idea we were discussing the finer points of shipping methods. When the policeman felt he had gotten all of his important eBay questions answered, he let us go. "I know you didn't do it on purpose," he said. That was the night eBay kept me out of jail.

That event reinforced for me the concept that eBay is everywhere. It is an unbelievable phenomenon that can help anyone anywhere find financial freedom and make their dreams come true. We have helped hundreds and hundreds of people get started, and nothing makes me happier than when I hear the success stories. They are the reason we do what we do.

A gentleman came to one of my seminars. He had lost his job because of cutbacks and was having an extremely difficult time making ends meet. The meager unemployment check he received every week offered only minimal assistance. After attending our seminar, he went to the unemployment office and stood in line. When he got to the front, he asked the woman behind the counter if starting an eBay business would disqualify him for unemployment. She told him it would not.

As a child, this gentleman collected coins. He had them in a vault and hadn't looked at them in years. He didn't even remember what he had. He emptied his safety deposit box and started his eBay business by selling his old coins. He earned $700 his first month, $1,600 his second month, and $3,000 the month after that. He is now a PowerSeller, currently earning his full-time income on eBay and, not to mention, netting almost twice as much as he made at the job he was laid off from.

Put this book down and make a beeline for your computer. Go into business for yourself tonight. Think outside the box and put the strategies and techniques you've learned here to work for you. eBay has provided the framework. Now, use it to make your dreams your reality.

Words of Wisdom

"To be yourself in a world that is constantly trying to make you something else is the greatest accomplishment."

—*Ralph Waldo Emerson*

Adam Ginsberg

Adam Ginsberg

Prompted to educate others with the knowledge and experience he has gained on eBay – Adam is a renowned speaker and educator throughout the US and Canada. An eBayer since 2001, he was named #1 New eBay Seller in 2002 and became a multi-million dollar seller on eBay with his "zStores".

Born and raised in New York, Adam is a graduate of Tulane University. With a diverse background in entrepreneurial businesses, Adam learned through experience how to create extraordinary success by establishing his businesses on eBay. His keen desire to share this success with others, led him to document and record his step-by-step formulas and to create his own easy-to-use training materials so others can learn How to Buy, Sell and Profit on eBay.

Adam has also established the "High Five Academy", a resource of educational seminars and materials for accelerated learning and success on eBay.

Adam draws significantly from his own inspirational success story to educate and inspire his audiences. The media has featured him in *Billiard Digest*, *Kiplinger*, *Entrepreneur* and *Fortune* magazines.
He has also been interviewed on *CNBC with David Faber* and *ABC World News Tonight with Peter Jennings*.

A d a m G i n s b e r g . c o m

Are You Ready To Take Action on eBay?

Adam Ginsberg can help you create a profitable eBay business of your own